ESSENTIAL
EGYPT

Original text by Sylvie Franquet and Anthony Sattin

Revised and updated by Sylvie Franquet

ISBN 978-0-7495-7083-5

Published by AA Publishing, a trading name of AA Media Limited, whose registered office is Fanum House, Basing View, Basingstoke, Hampshire RG21 4EA. Registered number 06112600.

A CIP catalogue record for this book is available from the British Library

Colour separation: AA Digital Department

Printed and bound in Italy by Printer Trento S.r.l.

Find out more about AA Publishing and the wide range of services the AA provides by visiting our website at theAA.com/shop

A04463

Maps in this title produced from mapping © Freytag-Berndt u. Artaria KG, 1231 Vienna-Austria

Additional data from Mountain High Maps® Copyright © 1993 Digitial Wisdom, Inc

About this book

This book is divided into five sections.

The essence of Egypt pages 6–19
Introduction; Features; Food and drink; Short break including the 10 Essentials

Planning pages 20–33
Before you go; Getting there; Getting around; Being there

Best places to see pages 34–55
The unmissable highlights of any visit to Egypt

Best things to do pages 56–75
Good places to have lunch; top activities; best markets; stunning views; places to take the children; best museums and more

Exploring pages 76–185
The best places to visit in Egypt, organized by area

Maps

All map references are to the maps on the covers. For example, Abydos has the reference 🔡 15L – indicating the grid square in which it is to be found

Admission prices

Inexpensive (under 25LE)
Moderate (25LE–60LE)
Expensive (more than 60LE)

Hotel prices

Prices are per room per night:
£ budget (under 350LE);
££ moderate (350LE–800LE);
£££ expensive (more than 800LE)

Restaurant prices

Prices are for a three-course meal per person without drinks:
£ budget (under 150LE);
££ moderate (150LE–300LE);
£££ expensive (more than 300LE)

Contents

BEST THINGS TO DO

56 – 75

EXPLORING...

76 – 185

The essence of...

Egypt boasts three of the greatest cities the world has known: pharaonic Thebes (Luxor), so important that the Egyptians simply called it "the City", ancient Alexandria (Al Iskandaria), the great centre of classical learning, and Cairo (Al Qahira), Africa's largest city and legendary "mother of the world". Three deserts make up the bulk of the country, forbidding places that still fill most Egyptians with horror. The Nile, the world's longest river, runs straight through it, making the land habitable. Finally there is that unique, rich and sensual light, which endows Egypt and its people with a touch of brilliance.

features

The dry desert climate has so perfectly preserved Egypt's monuments, representing more than 5,000 years of history, that there is no shortage of things to see. In the past the usual route for travellers was to arrive in Cairo, then travel up the Nile to Luxor and Aswan. However, most now head for the beaches of Sinai or the Red Sea coast, and see the antiquities of Luxor, ancient Thebes, on a day trip. The more adventurous travel further south along the Red Sea towards the Sudanese border, or make trips to the oases in the Western Desert.

GEOGRAPHY

● About 90 per cent of Egypt's approximately 1 million sq km (386,000sq miles) is desert, much of it low-lying, but also containing mountains, the highest being Gebel Katarina in Sinai (2,642m/8,668ft).

● The majority of people live on 33,000sq km (12,740 sq miles) of flat, fertile land along the Nile.

POPULATION

● The population of Egypt is now around 80 million, and it is growing at about 2 per cent each year, with 30 per cent of the population under 15.

● Greater Cairo has close to 18 million inhabitants, and some parts

have the highest population density in the world.

- Women account for 69 per cent of people who can't read in Egypt, where one in four are illiterate.
- Some 90 per cent of Egyptians are Sunni Muslim, while most of the rest are Coptic Christians, with a small minority of Jewish people and other Christians.
- Many Egyptians in the north have Greek and European features; in the south there is a distinctive Nubian influence, and the Bedouin have Semitic Arab features.

ECONOMIC FACTORS

- Oil production, revenue from the Suez Canal, tourism and money sent home by Egyptian workers abroad account for the majority of foreign currency earnings.
- Some 32 per cent of Egyptians work in agriculture, 20 per cent in tourism.
  - Officially, 10.7 per cent of the population is unemployed, but it is believed it could even be as high as 20 per cent.
  - Around 20 per cent of Egyptians live below the poverty line, and another 25 per cent are only just above it.

TOURISM

- In 2008, 13 million tourists visited Egypt. The government is hoping to increase numbers to 16 million by 2014.

food & drink

Wall paintings in ancient Egyptian tombs show large banquets with mounds of food and the pharaohs' descendants seem keen to carry on this tradition. Egyptian food is simple but tasty, at its best when it comes as a table filled with *mezze* to be shared with friends.

NATIONAL DISHES

Egyptian cuisine reflects the many foreign invasions of the country, with European, Lebanese and Turkish influences. *Mezze* (appetisers) are a good introduction to Egyptian food. Often to accompany drinks or as a starter, a number of small dishes are put in the middle of the table to be scooped up with *aish baladi* (flat pitta bread). The most popular are *wara'a aynab* (stuffed vine leaves), *tahina*

(sesame paste), *baba ghanoug* (mashed aubergine with *tahina*), hummus (chickpea puree) and fresh salads.

Stewed *fuul*, or fava beans, is definitely the most common dish, eaten at breakfast and throughout the day. The beans are stewed for about 12 hours, traditionally using the heat from the hammam (steam bath). Egyptians believe that eating too

much *fuul* is bad for the brain and the *fuul* diet is often cited as the cause for the nation's woes, from the lethargy of the bureaucrats to the crazy driving. *Fuul* often comes with more beans, this time mashed, rolled into balls and fried, called *taamiya*. Vegetarians or carbohydrate fanatics love *kushari*, a mixture of macaroni, rice, fried onions, chickpeas and lentils, topped with a spicy tomato sauce. More elaborate is *meloukhiya*, a spinach-like vegetable made into a thick soup with garlic, rabbit or chicken. Chicken and red meat are usually grilled, most often as

kebab (lamb or beef skewers) or *kofta* (meatballs). Pigeon *(hamam)* is a delicacy, especially stuffed with wheat and fenugreek.

SWEETS

The most popular oriental pastries are *basbousa* (oven-baked semolina cake soaked in honey), *baqlawa* (filo pastry stuffed with nuts and honey) and *kunafa* (shredded and spun wheat pastry) stuffed either with thick cream, cream cheese or nuts). The best of Egyptian desserts is *Umm Ali*, a rich mixture of cracker bread, coconut, cream, nuts

and raisins, soaked in hot milk. *Roz bi-laban* (rice pudding), *mahallabiya* (cornflour pudding) and crème caramel are standards on menus.

CAFE PLEASURES

Tea is a good thirst quencher, even in the heat, and Arabian coffee with sugar *(qahwa mazbout)* soon becomes a habit, but cafes have other pleasures to offer. All year round there are fresh fruit juices, as well, a wide selection of soft

drinks. Egyptians claim that "once you drink from the Nile you will always come back", but it is wiser to stick to bottled mineral water. Traditional cafes also serve herbal infusions such as *yansoon* (anis), *helba* (fenugreek), *karkadeh* (hibiscus) and *'irfa* (cinnamon), and in winter try *sahlab*, a creamy concoction of arrowroot and cinnamon, usually topped with nuts and coconut.

ALCOHOLIC DRINKS

Although many Egyptians, as Muslims, do not drink alcohol, it is usually available wherever tourism is well established. Locally brewed Stella and Saqqara beers are very drinkable and some imported beers are available. The quality of Egyptian wine has improved over the last few years, and it comes in red, white, rosé and now even has a sparkling version. Most imported wines are sold at inflated prices, even in tax-free shops. Avoid local impersonations of famous-brand spirits – Johnny Talker, Marcel Horse and Ricardo.

short break

If you only have a short time and would like to take home some unforgettable memories, you can do something local and capture the real flavour of the country. These suggestions will give you a range of sights and experiences that won't take long, won't cost very much and will make your visit very special.

● **See the pyramids at Giza** (► 38–39) – they are, quite simply, wonders of the ancient world.

● **Watch a belly dancer** to understand the sensual rhythm of the people and to tune your ear to the sounds of Egypt's traditional music.

● **Snorkel or dive in the Red Sea** (► 66) to glimpse the corals and colourful fish, but remember to leave them as you found them.

● **Explore the varied, desert** which makes up more than nine-tenths of the country.

● **Sail the Nile on a felucca** listening to the water against the prow, the boatman's song and the sound of villagers along the shore.

● **Visit a mosque** – all but two of Egypt's mosques are open to tourists. Some are among the country's most stunning buildings.

● **Bargain in the souks,** remembering to pit your wits – and humour – against the salesman's wiles and hospitality.

● **Marvel at the pharaohs' treasures** in museums throughout the country, but especially in Cairo's Egyptian Museum (► 48–49) and the Luxor Museum (► 144).

● **Linger over a mint tea** or smoke a water pipe in a cafe for a glimpse into Egyptian daily life.

● **Wander around Karnak** (➤ 44–45) in the early morning, and discover the ultimate expression of the power, the skills, the sense of beauty and the religious fervour of the ancient Egyptians.

Planning

Before you go

WHEN TO GO

JAN	FEB	MAR	APR	MAY	JUN	JUL	AUG	SEP	OCT	NOV	DEC
18°C	21°C	23°C	27°C	32°C	34°C	35°C	35°C	32°C	30°C	23°C	18°C
64°F	70°F	73°F	81°F	90°F	93°F	95°F	95°F	90°F	86°F	73°F	64°F

High season   Low season

Temperatures are the average daily maximum in Cairo. Temperatures in Alexandria and on the Mediterranean coast are similar in winter, but during summer the average is 5°C (7°F) lower; in Aswan, temperatures are on average 5–8°C (7–12°F) higher than Cairo, but during winter they plummet at night and it can be bitterly cold. Alexandria receives the most rain and Cairo sees a little during winter, but it hardly ever rains in the south. Between March and April the *khamaseen*, a hot, dry and often very strong wind, blows in dust from the Western Desert. The best months to visit are October and November, February and March. December and January are high season, and are best for visiting the south. July and August are scorching anywhere away from the Mediterranean.

WHAT YOU NEED

● Required
○ Suggested
▲ Not required

Some countries require a passport to remain valid for a minimum period (usually at least six months) beyond the date of entry—contact their consulate or embassy or your travel agency for details.

	UK	Germany	USA	Netherlands	Spain
Passport	●	●	●	●	●
Visa (regulations can change—check before making reservations)	●	●	●	●	●
Onward or return ticket	▲	▲	▲	▲	▲
Health inoculations (Hepatitis A and B, Rabies, Typhoid and others)	○	○	○	○	○
Health documentation (➤ 23, Health Insurance)	▲	▲	▲	▲	▲
Travel insurance	○	○	○	○	○
Driving licence (national)	●	●	●	●	●
Car insurance certificate (if own car)	●	●	●	●	●
Car registration document (if own car)	●	●	●	●	●

WEBSITES

Egyptian Ministry of Tourism: www.touregypt.net
Egyptian State Information Service: www.sis.gov.eg
Egyptian Tourist Authority: www.egypt.travel

TOURIST OFFICES AT HOME

In the UK

Egyptian Tourist Authority
Egyptian House, 170 Piccadilly
London W1V 9DD
☎ 020 7493 5282

In the USA

Egyptian Tourist Authority

8383 Wilshire Boulevard, Suite 215
Beverly Hills, Los Angeles
CA90211
☎ 323/653-8815

630 Fifth Avenue
Suite 1706, New York NY10111
☎ 212/332-2570

HEALTH INSURANCE

Egypt has well-qualified doctors and good hospitals, particularly in Cairo and Alexandria. Taking out travel insurance which covers medical care is a must. Keep all receipts and medical bills for reimbursement back home.

Have a dental check-up before leaving home. In an emergency contact your embassy for a list of English-speaking dentists. Hotels should also have a list, too. There are good dentists in Cairo and Alexandria, but treatment has to be paid for on the spot. Make sure you are covered by your medical insurance.

TIME DIFFERENCES

| GMT | Egypt | Germany | USA (NY) | Netherlands | Spain |
| 12 noon | 2PM | 1PM | 7AM | 1PM | 1PM |

Egypt stays two hours ahead of GMT (Greenwich Mean Time) most of the year, except during summer time (beginning of May to beginning of October), when it is three hours ahead. Time is a looser concept in Egypt than in Europe: five minutes can mean a few hours, and tomorrow can easily mean next week.

NATIONAL HOLIDAYS

1 Jan *New Year's Day*
7 Jan *Coptic Christmas Day*
April *Coptic Easter Sunday (day before Sham al Nessim)*
April *Sham al Nessim*
25 Apr *Liberation Day*

1 May *Labour Day*
23 Jul *Revolution Day*
6 Oct *Armed Forces Day*

The Islamic New Year, Prophet's Birthday, *Aid al Fitr* (3 days) and *Aid al Adha* (4 days) are also national holidays (dates vary). In addition, Egypt observes the traditional feast days of the Muslim Year and the month of fasting, Ramadan (► opposite).

WHAT'S ON WHEN

Islamic Festivals

The Islamic calendar is based on a lunar cycle of 12 months of 29 or 30 days, so the Muslim year is 11 days shorter than the Western calendar. This makes it difficult to give exact dates for Muslim festivals. To be sure, check details with the Egyptian Tourist Authority (www.egypt.travel).

Ras al Sana (Islamic New Year): first of the month of Muharram
Aid al Fitr: end of Ramadan.
Aid al Adha (Bayram): holiday when sheep are slaughtered to commemorate Abraham's sacrifice.

Moulids

Moulids, or celebrations of saints' days, take place throughout the year and throughout Egypt. The *Moulid al Nabi* (Birthday of the Prophet) is celebrated all over the country, especially near the al Husayn Mosque (► 96) in Cairo. The most important *moulids* such as *al Husayn* and *Sayyida Zeinab* in Cairo, *Sayyid al Badawi* in Tanta and *Abu al Haggag* in Luxor attract thousands and sometimes millions of believers from all over Egypt and the Islamic world. There are also a few Coptic *moulids* and one Jewish *moulid.*

January 7 Jan: Coptic Christmas after 43 days of abstaining from animal products.
End of Jan–beginning Feb: Cairo International Book Fair.

February International Fishing Competition that takes place in Hurghada.
22 Feb: dawn rays of the sun reach the sanctuary at Abu Simbel temple.
Luxor Marathon: popular annual event.
Nitaq Festival: downtown Cairo festival of art, theatre and poetry.

March/April Coptic Easter: date varies up to five weeks after Western Easter.
Sham al Nessim: public holiday the Monday after Coptic Easter, dating from pharaonic times, celebrating the onset of spring.

June International Festival of Oriental Dance in Cairo
(www.nilegroup.net).

September International Festival for Experimental Theatre in Cairo
(tel: 02-285 4509).
Alexandria International Film Festival (http://alexfilmfest.tripod.com).

October After the cotton harvest, *moulid* of Sayyid al Badawi in Tanta.
Pharaoh's Rally (www.rallyedespharaons.it).
22 Oct: dawn rays of the sun reach the sanctuary at Abu Simbel temple.

November Arabic Music Festival: 10 days of classical and traditional Arabic music at the Cairo Opera House.
4 Nov: Luxor Festival (dance and music).

December Cairo International Film Festival (www.cairofilmfestival.com).
International Nile Regatta Festival in Cairo and Luxor (tel: 02-393 4350).

Ramadan
During the month of Ramadan, most Muslim Egyptians abstain from drinking, eating, smoking and other pleasures from sunrise to sunset. Businesses work more or less part time and the traffic becomes absolutely frantic in the hour before sunset, as everyone tries to get home to break the fast. In the evening families go to the area around al Husayn Mosque in Cairo for amusement, tea and a waterpipe. Bars, if open at all, don't serve alcohol to Egyptians, not even to Copts, and it is advisable to take your passport for this reason.

Getting there

BY AIR

Cairo International Airport

🚉 N/A

🚌 45 minutes

🚗 30–60 minutes

20km (12.5 miles) to city centre

Luxor International Airport

🚉 N/A

🚌 N/A

🚗 15 minutes

7km (4.5 miles) to city centre

The national airline, EgyptAir (tel: 02-2483 0888 or national call centre 0900 70000; www.egyptair.com), operates direct flights from most European capitals and the US to Cairo, as well as some flights direct to Luxor and Alexandria. Several European airlines offer direct flights to Cairo, including BA (tel: 02-2480 0380, www.britishairways.com), Air France (tel: 02-2770 6252; www.airfrance.com) and KLM (tel: 02-5805700, www.klm.com). Most travellers enter Egypt through its main airport, Cairo International Airport, and some through Alexandria, Luxor or Sharm el Sheikh.

Cairo International Airport (www.cairo-airport.com) is 20km (12.5 miles) northeast of the city centre. Terminal 2 is closed for renovation at the time of writing, so all flights arrive and depart from Terminal 1 (flight enquiries tel: 09007 7777/2777). There are ATMs, a tourist office and exchange offices, and free WiFi in Terminal 1. The easiest way to get into town is by taxi, which is relatively inexpensive. There is an affordable, no-hassle, fixed-price limousine service in the Arrivals hall. Depending on traffic, travel time can be between 30 minutes and over an hour to the Downtown area. A new Cairo Airport Shuttle Bus operates to Heliopolis and Downtown (35LE), Giza, Mohandeseen and Zamalek (40LE), and Maadi and the Pyramid area (40LE). Buses leave every half hour and should be pre-booked from the counter in the Arrivals Hall (tel: 02-2265

3937). AC bus 356 runs every 20 minutes to Midan Tahrir in the centre of Cairo, as does the public bus 400, 24 hours a day.

Luxor International Airport is 7km (4.5 miles) east of town. There is no public transport, but plenty of taxis. Bargaining over the price is essential.

Aswan International Airport is 25km (15.5 miles) southwest of the city, and only taxis are available.

Alexandria's al Nozha Airport is currently closed for renovations, and flights now land at Borg Al Arab Airport, about 40km (25 miles) southwest of the city. A bus leaves for the airport in front of the Cecil Hotel in Alexandria three hours before all departures, and brings arrivals into town from the airport. Bus 475 goes between the airport and Misr Station.

Sharm el Sheikh International Airport is 10km (6 miles) north of Naama Bay, and only taxis are available.

BY LAND

Egypt has two official borders with Israel and the Palestinian Territories at Rafah and Taba. The border crossing in Rafah is open at the time of writing, but for special cases only. The security situation remains volatile, so check beforehand if you intend to cross there. The crossing at Taba, a few kilometres from Eilat in Israel, has remained open. Four East Delta buses a day leave Cairo from the main Turgoman bus station to Taba (5 hours), as well as shared taxis. In Taba passengers walk 600m (660 yards) to the border, and another 150m (165 yards) across to the Israeli side. On the Israeli side, local bus 15 connects to Eilat's Central Bus Station, from where there are hourly buses to Tel Aviv and Jerusalem.

BY SEA

There are two fast ferries between Nuweiba and Aqaba (www.abmaritime.com.jo/main.html). At the time of writing there are no ferries between Egypt and European ports. The Nile River Valley Transport Corporation (tel: 02-575 9058) has a weekly ferry from Wadi Halfa to Aswan.

Getting around

PUBLIC TRANSPORT

Internal flights EgyptAir flies daily from Cairo to most of Egypt's main cities and can be booked through EgyptAir offices (tel: 02-2265 7256; www.egyptair.com).

Trains The Egyptian State Railway (www.egyptrail.gov.eg) serves the Nile Valley, Alexandria, Suez, Port Said and Mersa Matruh. Buy tickets in advance. Wagon-Lits (tel: 02-2576 1319) operates a sleeper train from Cairo to Luxor and Aswan, and fast trains to Alexandria. Book in advance, payments in cash (Euros or dollars), or with credit cards, at Abela Egypt Sleeping Train Ticket office, to the right of Ramses Station in Cairo (tel: 02-2574 9474; www.sleepingtrains.com).

Buses Buses run from Cairo to most cities in Egypt. Tickets for air-conditioned buses should be booked in advance. Buses leave from the Cairo Gateway (Turgoman Garage, Shari' al Gisr, Bulaq, 1km/0.6 miles north of Ramses station). Superjet and Golden Rocket operate fast buses to Alexandria and Marsa Matruh. All Sinai buses (East Delta Travel; tel: 02-2574 2814) leave from Cairo Gateway, as do the buses for the South, the Western Oases and the Red Sea (all Upper Egypt Bus Co; tel: 02-2576 0261). Buses for Al Faiyum leave from under Al Munib Bridge in Giza.

Urban transport Cairo's buses are packed full and women risk being hassled, so it is best to use taxis, which are cheap and more comfortable (look out for metered, air-conditioned taxis). The metro is easy to use, especially from Downtown Cairo to Coptic Cairo or Heliopolis.

TAXIS

Collective service taxis are usually faster than buses and charge similar rates to bus fares. They usually operate from near bus stations and leave as soon as they have six or seven passengers on board. Agree on a price before driving away.

FARES AND TICKETS

Students and youths Most museums and sights offer a 50 per cent reduction on tickets and there are considerable reductions on rail and airline tickets for students who have an official student card. An ISIC Student Card can be issued at the Egyptian Student Travel Services (23 Shari' al Manyal, Roda Island, Cairo; tel: 02-2531 0330; www.estsegypt.com). You need one passport photo and a student card or letter from your university or college proving you are a student.

Senior citizens There are no special concessions for senior citizens.

DRIVING

- The Egyptians drive on the right side of the road.
- Seatbelts are compulsory.
- There are many petrol *(benzeen)* stations in the main towns, but fewer out in the countryside. Petrol stations are serviced, not self-serve. Always fill your tank to the limit, and clean the oil filter regularly, as dust and impurities in the petrol tend to clog up the engine. Larger petrol stations are often open until late at night. Petrol is cheaper than in Europe and the USA.
- Speed limits are as follows:
  On all highways 100kph (62mph)
  On main roads 90kph (56mph)
  In urban centres 50kph (31mph)
- Avoid driving in the dark outside the city as some drivers do not use their lights or switch them on at the last minute, blinding you. Just after sunset people walk their animals home and there is general chaos on rural roads.
- Egyptian car mechanics are often masters of invention and can usually be relied upon to fix a broken-down car. There are also usually people at hand to help you push your car to the next garage or to the side of the road. Most garages stock a good range of spare parts.

CAR RENTAL

Cairo traffic and Egyptian road manners are daunting, but now that traffic restrictions have been lifted, it can be fun to rent a car. It is best to use an international company, and book it on the web before arrival. You will need an International driving licence. Alternatively, book a car with a driver.

Being there

TOURIST OFFICES

Alexandria
Midan Saad Zaghloul ☎ 03-485 1556
Misr Railway Station ☎ 03-492 5985

Aswan
Midan al Mahatta, next to the train station ☎ 097-231 2811

Cairo
5 Shari' Adly, Downtown ☎ 02-2391 3454
Ramses Railway Station ☎ 02-2579 0767
Giza Pyramids ☎ 02-3383 8823

Cairo International Airport ☎ 02-2265 3642

Hurghada
Resort Strip ☎ 065-344 4420

Luxor
Midan al Mahatta, opposite the station ☎ 095-237 3294
Luxor Airport ☎ 095-237 2306

Port Said
Shari' Filastin 8 ☎ 066-323 5289

Siwa
SiwaTown ☎ 046-460 1338

MONEY

The Egyptian pound (LE, *guineh* in Arabic) is divided into 100 piastres (PT, *irsh* in Arabic). There are notes for 25 and 50 piastres and 1, 5, 10, 20, 50 and 100 pounds, and coins for 50 piastres and 1 pound. Traveller's cheques, preferably in US$, can be changed in banks and exchange bureaux (transaction charge). Credit cards are widely accepted at banks, hotels and upmarket restaurants, but check first. Many five-star hotels and banks in resorts have automatic cash dispensing machines.

TIPS/GRATUITIES

Yes ✓   No ✗

Restaurants (service not included)	✓	10%
Cafes/bars	✓	10%
Taxis (negotiate the price first or use meter)	✓	5–10%
Chambermaids	✓	15–20LE
Porters	✓	10–20LE
Museum and site guides	✓	10–20LE
Toilets	✓	1–5LE

POSTAL AND INTERNET SERVICES

Stamps can be bought at post offices, souvenir shops and hotel newsagents. Airmail letters take about a week to arrive in Europe, a little longer for the USA and Australia. Post your letters in your hotel or use a post office; avoid street letterboxes. Cairo's main post office (open 24 hours) is on Midan al Ataba. Internet is readily available in many hotels. In more touristy areas, there are often several internet cafes to choose from.

TELEPHONES

Local calls can be made from coin-operated phone boxes, hotels and kiosks. International calls can be made from Telephone and Telegraph (TT) offices. The main branches, at Midan al Tahrir and at 8 Shari' Adly, are open 24 hours, while other branches are open 7am–10pm daily.

International dialling codes

From Egypt to:
UK: 00 44
Germany: 00 49
USA: 00 1
Netherlands: 00 31
Spain: 00 34

Emergency telephone numbers

Police: 122
Tourist police: 126 or 02-395 9116
Fire: 180
Ambulance: 123
Anglo-American hospital in Cairo:
02-735 6162

EMBASSIES AND CONSULATES

UK ☎ 02-2791 6000
Germany ☎ 02-2728 2000
Netherlands ☎ 02-2739 5500

Spain ☎ 02-2735 6462
US ☎ 02-2797 3300

HEALTH ADVICE

Sun advice Use a high-factor sunscreen or sunblock, cover up with light cotton clothes, wear sun glasses and a hat when out in the sun. Coffee and alcohol are dehydrating; instead drink plenty of water.

Drugs Pharmacists (*Saydaliya* in Arabic) usually speak English and can recommend treatment for minor ailments. A wide range of drugs is available over the counter and they are cheap. Check the expiry date.

Safe water It is reasonably safe to drink tap water in the main cities, but it is advisable to buy bottled water, which is widely available. Drink at least 3 litres of water a day to avoid dehydration. Avoid ice cubes in drinks.

PERSONAL SAFETY

Petty crime remains rare in Egypt, but like everywhere else you should watch your belongings in busy tourist areas and on full buses.

● Leave money and valuables in the hotel safe. Carry only what you need.

● There is a crackdown on drugs, with fines for possession, and life imprisonment or hanging for anyone convicted of dealing or smuggling.

● There are roadblocks in the main cities at night. Tourist Police assistance: ☎ 126/122

Safety in Middle Egypt

Although it is no longer necessary to travel with police convoy in most of Egypt, there is still a threat from terrorism and security is tight, especially in resort areas. Since President Mubarak's resignation and at the time of writing, the situation for tourists is calm but travel advice and safety precautions are subject to change. Check governmental advice before travelling: www.fco.gov.uk.

ELECTRICITY

The power supply in Egypt is 220 volts. Sockets take two-round-pin plugs. British visitors will need an adaptor, US visitors a voltage transformer.

OPENING HOURS

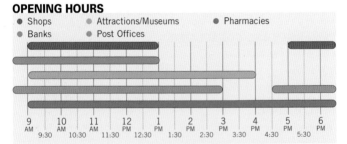

In tourist areas shops stay open all day until late in high season. In Ramadan everything tends to open an hour later and close earlier, but shops reopen 8–10pm. Banks in tourist areas may stay open all day, until late. Banks at Cairo Airport and Marriott and Nile Hilton hotels in Cairo are open 24 hours. Museums and monuments close on Friday 11–1 (12–2, summer). Post offices are open Sat–Thu. Pharmacies are often open until 9pm. Summer opening times run May–Sep and winter Oct–Apr.

LANGUAGE

The official language in Egypt is Arabic, but English is widely taught in schools. People are always happy, and proud, to practise their foreign languages, but even if you only speak a few words in Arabic you will generally meet with an enthusiastic response. Egyptians elaborate their greetings to each other, even on the telephone, and their love of language and for joking with words is legendary in the Arab world. The following is a phonetic transliteration from the Arabic script.

hotel	*funduq/otel*	shower	*dush*
single/double room	*oda single/dubbel*	bathroom	*hammam*
one night	*layla wahda*	air-conditioning	*takyeef*
I have a reservation	*'andi hagz*	telephone	*telefun*
hot water	*mayya sokhna*	key	*muftah*
bank	*bank*	Egyptian pound	*guineh*
where is the bank?	*feen al bank?*	British pound	*guineh sterlini*
I want to change...	*ayyiz/ayza*	post office/mail	*bosta/barid*
	agghayyar...	cheque	*cheque*
	(male/female)	how much is...?	*bi kaam...?*
restaurant	*mat'am*	mineral water	*mayya ma'daniya*
bill	*al hisab*	menu	*cart/menu*
tea/coffee	*shay/qahwa*	wine red, white	*nabit ahmar, abyad*
bread	*'aysh*	beer	*beera*
right/left	*yimeen/shemaal*	the airport	*al mataar*
straight ahead	*ala toul*	I want a taxi	*ayiz/ayza taksi*
where is...?	*feyn...?*	when does the bus	*al utubees yisaafir*
the bus station	*mahattat al utubees*	leave?	*emta?*
the train station	*mahattat al atr*	...arrive	*...yawsal emta?*
yes/no	*aywa, na'am/la'a*	you're welcome	*'afwan*
please	*min fadlak (to a*	God willing	*inshallah*
	man), min fadlik	hello (to Muslims)	*as-salaamu 'alaykum*
	(to a woman)	hello (to Copts)	*sa'eeda*
thank you	*shukran*	goodbye	*ma'a salaama*

Best places to see

1 Abydos

Abydos, dedicated to the god Osiris, was a place of pilgrimage for almost two thousand years. Today it is one of the most remarkable archaeological sites.

Abydos is one of the oldest Egyptian settlements, founded long before the Dynastic period (3050BC), and for thousands of years it was a place of pilgrimage. According to legend, Osiris, god of the underworld, was buried here, and a gap in the nearby hills was the gateway to the underworld.

A burial in Abydos, therefore, was considered a good way of ensuring an after-life. Early Egyptian kings built symbolic graves in the desert and those who could were either buried there, had commemorative stones raised in their honour or had their mummies brought on a pilgrimage after their death.

Most of ancient Abydos has disappeared or is yet to be excavated. The main attraction is the Temple of Seti I, a magnificent white-marble building of the 14th century BC. There are many inscriptions and images, while reliefs on the walls of the Second Hypostyle Hall are among the finest of the New Kingdom, with a subtlety and vividness that was later lost.

The temple's outer hall and facade were finished by Seti's son, Ramses II, who also built a smaller temple some 300m (330yds) away (not always accessible). Before visiting that, however, go out of the back of the temple to the Osirion or Cenotaph, a strange subterranean building, now often submerged by rising ground-water. A sarcophagus was found here (although Seti was buried in the Valley of the Kings, ➤ 40–41), which was perhaps part of a ritual unification of the pharaoh and the god of the dead.

✚ 15L ✉ Al Araba al Madfuna, 10km (6 miles) southwest of Al Balyana ⏰ Daily 8–5 (4 Oct–Apr) ✋ Moderate
🍴 Osiris Park cafe 🚌 Luxor travel agency excursions and taxi are the preferred ways to get to Abydos or rent a car in Luxor as travel restrictions no longer apply

2 Al Ahram and Abu'l Hol (Pyramids and Sphinx)

The pyramids at Giza are the most instantly recognizable monuments in the world, while the nearby Sphinx retains its aura of mystique.

More than 80 pyramids line the west bank of the Nile between Giza and Al Faiyum, but the three large pyramids at Giza are by far the most impressive. It is easy to trace the fascinating development of the pyramids from the beginning with Djoser's step pyramid at Saqqara (➤ 102), through Snefru's pyramids at Dahshur (➤ 98) to the geometrically perfect Great Pyramid of Khufu (Cheops), built at the apogee of Old Kingdom power. Khufu's was the first of the three main pyramids to be built and is the largest, originally 146.6m (480ft) high (now shrunk to 137.5m/451ft). His son Khafre (Chephren) built the Second Pyramid (136.4m/447ft high) and gave the Sphinx his face, while Khafre's son Menkaure (Mycerinus) built the third, only 62m (203ft) high. Around each pyramid there are the remains of the smaller pyramids of the royal families.

If there is still no complete answer to the question of how the pyramids were built, then the Sphinx is shrouded in even more mystery. The massive statue cut out of the living rock has a lion's body and a man's head, believed to be that of the Pharaoh Khafre, to whose pyramid it was connected by a causeway. A lot of effort is going into protecting the plateau from damage and from the touts. As a result most of the hassle now happens before you arrive, but go straight to the ticket office to avoid it all. The new Grand Egyptian Museum is under construction on the edge of the Giza Plateau and is expected to open in 2012.

✚ 6C ✉ Giza plateau, 16km (10 miles) southwest of Cairo 🕐 Giza plateau daily 8–6 in summer; 8–4 in winter. Solar Boat Museum May–Oct 9–5; Nov–Apr 9–4 💰 Giza plateau and Sphinx expensive; extra ticket to enter the Pyramid of Khufu expensive; Pyramid of Khafre moderate; Pyramid of Menkaure inexpensive 🍴 Cafe (£) near Sphinx, restaurant (££–£££) at Mena House Hotel 🚌 Bus 355 and 357 from Midan Tahrir; minibus 82 ❓ *Son et lumière* show in several languages at the Sphinx daily ☎ 02-3385 2880 ❓ 150 tickets for Khufu Pyramid go on sale at 7:30am, another 150 at 1pm

3 Biban al Muluk (Valley of the Kings)

www.thebanmappingproject.com

For 500 years some of Egypt's most famous pharaohs were buried in splendour in fascinating tombs hidden in the Valley of the Kings.

One of the high points of ancient Egyptian history occurred when the princes of Thebes (Luxor) established what is known as the New Kingdom (1570–1070BC). Previous pharaohs had been buried in easy-to-rob pyramids so Theban pharaohs, who believed their future life depended on keeping their mummies and grave goods intact, had themselves buried in the hills. The tombs were cut out of the rock and some are master-pieces of engineering: Seti I's tomb is 100m (330ft) long, while KV5, the tomb of the sons of Ramses II, has revealed more than a hundred chambers. The walls were covered with intricate inscriptions and decorations and the tombs were filled with precious objects, protected by deep pits and hidden beneath rubble. All were broken into in antiquity.

Seti I's tomb is considered to be the finest in the valley, by those who have been lucky enough to see it – it is now indefinitely closed (Horemheb's No 57 is similar in design, if not decor).

Tombs are regularly closed and numbers are often restricted, as in Tutankhamun's, to minimize damage. The boy-king's tomb is of interest because of the romance surrounding its discovery and because the mummy is still there. After the tomb was opened by Howard Carter in 1922, several people who visited the site or were involved in its discovery died mysteriously, said to be caused by the curse of the pharaoh.

Among the more heavily decorated tombs are those of Ramses IV (No 2), Ramses VI (No 9), and Ramses III (No 11), while that of Tuthmosis III (No 34), high up the valley, is the most challenging to reach.

🕈 16M ⊠ West Bank, beyond Al Gurna
🕘 Daily 6–4 (6–5 Jun–Sep) ✋ Entrance to three tombs expensive; extra ticket for tomb of Tutankhamun expensive 🚌 Taxis only, or rented bicycles ❓ Tickets are sold at the back of the visitors' centre of the Valley of the Kings. Inside the site you can just buy the extra ticket for the tomb of Tutankhamun
🛈 Midan al Mahatta, Luxor; tel: 095-237 3942

4 Deir Sant Katarin (St Catherine's Monastery)

www.st-katherine.net

The monastery is supposedly built on the site of the burning bush from which God spoke to Moses. Pilgrims also climb Mount Sinai, where Moses is believed to have received the Ten Commandments.

According to the scriptures, when Moses went up towards Mount Sinai to receive the Ten Commandments, God spoke to him through a burning bush. The monastery was founded on the supposed site of the bush in AD527, on the orders of Byzantine Emperor Justinian. It is named after St Catherine, the martyr from Alexandria who, after being tortured on a spiked wheel, was transported by angels to the nearby Gebel Katerina. The monastery's icon collection is one of the most important in the world, covering 1,400 years of

painting, including the period when Byzantine Christians were banned from producing images of the Holy Family or saints (AD 746–842).

Icons are shown in the narthex of the main church, an original Justinian granite building that incorporates the Chapel of the Burning Bush. Inside the church, icons of the saints are hung on and around 12 magnificent pillars and candles are lit under their images on their name day. The iconostasis (altar screen) is a later 17th-century work, but beyond it in the sanctuary there is one of the masterpieces of Byzantine art, a 6th-century mosaic of the Transfiguration. Outside the church a bush grows which, in spite of local legend, is not the one mentioned in the Bible.

✚ 11F ✉ Sinai desert, 450km (280 miles) from Cairo, 140km (87 miles) from Dahab ☎ 0693-470 353 (Monastery guest house) ◷ Mon–Thu, Sat 9–11:45. Closed Fri, Sun and religious hols ⛊ Free, inexpensive to visit Monastery Treasury 🍴 Cafe/restaurant (£) 🚌 East Delta buses from Cairo, Sharm el Sheikh, Dahab and Nuweiba to the village, 2km (1.2 miles) from the monastery. Taxi to monastery or pleasant walk ✈ EgyptAir flights to Sharm el Sheikh from Cairo ❓ Special permission is needed to visit the Chapel of the Burning Bush

5 # Karnak

No other ancient religious centre matches Karnak for scale and grandeur. Here, for 1,500 years, the priests offered prayers to the god Amun.

Amun was the local god of Thebes long before the New Kingdom, but his status grew along with that of the Theban princes. By the end of the New Kingdom the priests of Amun owned huge estates and controlled shipping, farming and industry. Their empire within an empire was controlled from the precinct of Amun in Karnak and at its centre stood the temple, embellished over the centuries as pharaohs wished to show goodwill towards the god. The result is one of the world's most extraordinary religious sites.

Karnak is a complex with several temple compounds, which can be confusing and overwhelming to visit. After entering through the 43m-high (141ft) outer pylon, walk to the core of the complex, the Temple of Amun. Dedicated to the triad of Thebes, the gods Amun, Mut and Khonsu, it has a wonderful "forest" of pillars, built by Ramses II. Continuing straight through the halls you will come to the sanctuary where the image of Amun lived and where, as the images on the walls show, daily offerings were made. Retracing your steps, turn left

out of the inner sanctuary to the Cachette Court, and continue to the Sacred Lake. From here, on the *son et lumière* stand, you can see over the compound. If you have time, stroll through the Open Air Museum, the Northern Enclosure with the Temple of Mut, and the Southern Enclosure.

🕂 16M ✉ 2.5km (1.5 miles) north of Luxor centre
🕐 Daily 6–5 (open till 6 May–Sep) 💷 Expensive
🍴 Cafe (£) by the Sacred Lake 🚌 Minibuses from Luxor centre ❓ *Son et lumière* show (a walking tour of the temple) 3 or 4 times nightly (tel: 095-238 6000; www.soundandlight.com.eg)
ℹ Corniche al Nil, Luxor ☎ 095-237 3294

6 Khan al Khalili, Cairo

The warren of alleys brings a touch of the Arabian nights to Cairo, in which shopping is just part of the sensory adventure.

The original *khan* (merchants' inn and storehouse) was built in 1382 and quickly became the focus of the city's international trade. Although it was reconstructed in the 16th century, something of the spirit of the original place is still there, as people from all over the world meet to talk and trade.

Officially Khan al Khalili now refers to a single street, but generally the term is used for the shopping area between the Mosque of Sayyidna al

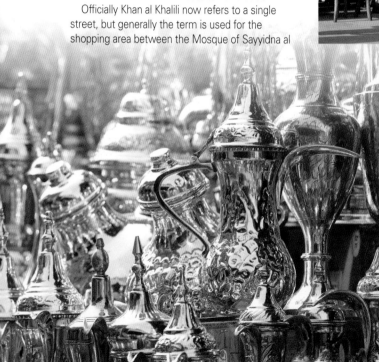

Husayn (➤ 96–97) and Muizz li-Din Allah, one of the Islamic city's main streets. The main alley connecting them, Al Badestan, is typical with its mix of cheap souvenirs and treasures, where imported Chinese junk sits alongside expensive jewellery and Lalique glass. In a smaller alley to the left of Al Badestan, coming from Al Husayn, Fishawi's cafe claims not to have closed since 1773 – not quite true, as you might find, but it is one of the area's social centres.

In the alleys of the Khan al Khalili there are silversmiths, copper beaters, leather workers and carpet sellers. At the bottom of Al Badestan, turn right onto the street of Muizz Lidin Allah, which leads to the old souk al Nahassin (the copper and gold market) where you can buy wonderful copper trays and gold jewellery. Heading the other way along this extraordinary street, past the old baths, an alley running alongside the Mosque of Barsbay leads past kohl and perfume sellers to the spice market.

✚ *Cairo 5d* ✉ Off Shari' al Azhar and Shari' al Muski
🕐 Morning to evening (some shops closed Fri prayers and Sun) 🍴 Several cafes and restaurants (£–££)
🚌 Buses from Midan Tahrir ❓ The cafes around Midan al Husayn are popular in the evening for a mint tea or a waterpipe; the bazaar is especially crowded on Fri afternoons and during religious hols
ℹ️ 5 Shari' Adly, Downtown; tel: 02-2391 3454

Al Mathaf al Masri (Egyptian Museum), Cairo

www.egyptianmuseum.gov.eg

The Egyptian Museum is one of the world's great storehouses of antiquities, and a visit is essential for understanding the glory of the ancient Egyptians.

Only part of the museum's collection is on display, but what is there is more than you could take in during a single visit. The ground-floor galleries are laid out in rough chronological order (though not numerically: No 1 is not the oldest), allowing you to walk clockwise from the entrance and have an overview of 3,000 years of Egyptian art.

The atrium has a few of the museum's masterpieces, including the Narmer Palette from 3100BC. The sculptures of the Old Kingdom are spectacular, particularly the wooden statue of Ka-Aper and the painted limestone scribe, both in

Room 42, and the statues of Rahotep and Nofret, and the dwarf Seneb with his family in Room 32.

The upper floor is devoted to treasures, most found in tombs. The staircase in Gallery 1 leads directly to the treasures of

Tutankhamun. Here, filling several galleries, are the 1,700 grave goods found in his tomb, from the solid gold mask to thrones, headrests, exquisite boxes and a series of golden chariots. The Tutankhamun treasures can overwhelm, but save some energy for other galleries, which are arranged according to subjects, from models (boats, farming scenes, warriors) to the lifelike Graeco-Roman portraits (Room 14). The mummies of several important pharaohs, including Ramses II, are on show in Room 52 (separate ticket required). A larger, high-tech Grand Egyptian Museum is under construction on the Giza Plateau (➤ 39) will not be complete until 2012.

✚ *Cairo 3d* ✉ Midan al Tahrir, Cairo ☎ 02-2579 6748 🕙 Daily 9–6:45 💶 Expensive; extra ticket for royal mummies expensive 🍴 Museum cafe (£) 🚇 Sadat 🚌 Many buses to Midan al Tahrir

49

8 Al Nil (the Nile)

This great river may no longer be Egypt's communication nerve, but it is still the country's lifeline.

The Nile is the world's longest river and one of the most beautiful. For the last half of its course it receives neither tributaries nor regular rainfall, yet in midsummer every year it used to rise in Egypt until it burst its banks and flooded the valley. Villages were built on mounds and ancient writers described them as looking like islands. When the river finally subsided, it left a thick deposit of mud on the land, producing fertile ground on which seeds were immediately planted. Some years the river rose so high it destroyed villages and towns, while in others it didn't rise high enough to produce a good crop and people went hungry. Ancient Egyptians worshipped the Nile as a god and hoped for its benevolence.

The source wasn't discovered until the 1850s, when British explorers Burton and Speke reached Lake Victoria. As a result of knowledge gained about the river, two dams were built (1902 and 1965) to control the flow of water to the valley. The dams and resultant Lake Nasser, the world's largest reservoir, have ended the flooding and made several crops a year possible, although the farmland is now suffering from a lack of fertilizing silt. With the Nile tamed and used almost exclusively by tourists and commuters, it is tempting to think that the river no longer has significance, but the Nile is as much a part of Egyptian life now as in ancient times.

Cruises on the Nile

A variety of boats sail on the Nile, from simple feluccas to five-star cruise-boats, but most offer the same itinerary. Sailing between Luxor and Aswan, they take in the sights in both towns and stop at the temples of Esna, Edfu and Kom Ombo on the way. Most take three or four days, although some take five and visit the temple of Dandara. Delays may occur at the narrow Esna lock, where boats often have to join a long queue waiting to pass through. The most romantic way to cruise the Nile is in a *dahabeyya*. Built in the style of the craft used by 19th-century travellers, these beautiful sailing boats can moor where they want, allowing passengers to see some of the smaller sights along the way.

✠ 6C–16Q

9 Philae Temples, Aswan

Philae reveals the glory of ancient Egypt's late flourish under the Greeks and Romans. It is also one of Egypt's most romantic sites.

The temples, shrines and kiosks of Philae Island were moved to the nearby Agilkia Island between 1972 and 1980 to protect them from the rising Nile water caused by the Aswan dams. As part of the massive operation Agilkia was shaped to make a replica of Philae Island. The main temple at Philae was dedicated to Osiris's wife Isis, who was worshipped throughout the Mediterranean world in Roman times and whose cult survived here until AD551, when it was replaced by that of the Virgin Mary.

Arriving at the island by boat is a wonderful experience. From the landing, colonnades lead up to the pylon of the Temple of Isis, which was built during the late Ptolemaic and early Roman era. The left-hand opening leads into a third-century-BC Birth House, dedicated to Horus, child

of Isis and Osiris. The main opening leads to a second pylon and the temple, which lost much of its decoration when it was converted into a church around AD553. The upper floor has interesting reliefs of Osiris, who was worshipped in mysterious rites here. The nearby Temple of Hathor, the deity associated with music, has a unique image of gods playing instruments. From the Kiosk of Trajan, originally built as a gateway to the island, there are beautiful views across the lake to the site of the original island, now submerged.

✚ 16Q ✉ Agilkia Island, 9km (5.5 miles) south of Aswan 🕐 Oct–May daily 7–4; Jun–Sep 7–5 🍴 Cafe (£) on the island 🚕 Taxi from Aswan 🛥 Regular boats from the riverbank ✋ Moderate–expensive ❓ Daily *son et lumière* show. Details at the site or tourist office; www.soundandlight.com.eg ℹ Corniche al Nil, Aswan; tel: 097-231 2811

10 Sultan Hasan Mosque-Madrasa, Cairo

The simple beauty and grand scale of this 14th-century mosque make it one of the most admired of Islamic monuments.

Sultan Hasan was the seventh of Sultan al Nasir Muhammad's eight sons and was 12 years old when he became sultan of Egypt in 1347. Four years later he was imprisoned in the *harem* by a

younger brother. After three years of *harem* life, he was restored to the throne, where he stayed for seven years before being murdered. In his life he knew wealth and debauchery, but Sultan Hasan will always be remembered for his teaching mosque *(madrasa)*, one of the largest and finest in the world.

The mosque was the centre of the community, accommodating students of four separate schools of Islamic law. The original design had four minarets but only three were built. One fell in 1361, killing many people; another fell in 1659 and was replaced by a smaller minaret. The sole survivor is 81.6m (267ft) high, one of the tallest in the city. The sultan intended to be buried here, but the tomb is empty, as his body disappeared. The tomb chamber is decorated with marble and wood, with a blue-and-gold wooden frieze around the room. The masterpiece, however, is the main prayer space, a massive, perfectly proportioned courtyard with four huge arches. Beautiful glass lamps, some now in the Museum of Islamic Art (▶ 90), were used to illuminate the prayer recesses. Opposite Sultan Hassan, built on a similar scale, is the 19th-century mosque of Al Rifai, where members of Egypt's former royal family are buried.

🕂 *Cairo 5e* ✉ Midan Salah al Din 🕗 Daily 8–5 (open till 6 Jun–Sep) 🖐 Inexpensive, tip for slippers 🍴 No cafe nearby, nearest in Khan al Khalili (▶ 46–47) 🚌 Minibus 54 from Midan al Tahrir

Best things to do

Good places to have lunch

Andrea (£–££)

Succulent slow-roast chicken and *mezze* in a peaceful garden.

✉ 59–60 Marioutiya Canal, Al Ahram, Giza ☎ 02-3383 1133

Aswan Moon (£–££)

Fresh juices, Nubian stews and salads while watching the river flow past. No alcohol served.

✉ Corniche al Nil, Aswan ☎ 097-231 6108

Citadel View (££)

Overlooking the stunning Al Azhar Park and all of the city, this beautiful restaurant with huge terrace serves good Egyptian food.

✉ Al Azhar Park, Shari' Salah Salem, Cairo ☎ 02-2510 9151

Fish Market (££–£££)

Excellent fish restaurant with great views of the Mediterranean.

✉ Corniche al Nil, beside the Kashafa Club, Alexandria ☎ 03-480 6597

Al Moudira (££–£££)

Delightful salads and Lebanese *mezze* served by the pool.

✉ Daba'iyya, West Bank, Luxor ☎ 012-325 1307; www.moudira.com

Naguib Mahfouz Coffee Shop (£)

Recover from shopping in the souks in this air-conditioned haven.

✉ 5 Al Bedestan alley, Khan al Khalili, Cairo ☎ 02-2590 3788

Oasis Café (£–££)

Stylish and peaceful cafe-restaurant in a gorgeous colonial building in the centre of town, with good Egyptian and international food.

✉ Shari' Dr Labib Habashi, Luxor ☎ 012-336 7121

Restaurant Mohammed (£–££)

Simple but very good food – choose from chicken, kebabs or local duck with rice and salad. Order in advance if you can.

✉ Gourna, near Pharaoh's Hotel, West Bank, Luxor ☎ 012-385 0227

Sofra (£–££)

Delicious Egyptian food served in a 19th-century house with a breezy roof terrace. No alcohol but great fresh juices.

✉ 90 Shari' Mohammed Farid, East Bank, Luxor ☎ 095-235 9752; www.sofra.com.eg

Tanta Waa Cafeteria & Restaurant (£–££)

This laid-back cafe overlooking the lovely spring serves great smoothies, salads and pasta dishes, and provides hammocks for an after-lunch snooze.

✉ Cleopatra's Bath, Siwa ☎ 010-472 9539

Top activities

Belly dance classes with Egypt's most famous belly dance teacher, Madame Raqia Hassan (tel: 02 3748 2338)

Birdwatching on Lake Qaraoun in Al Faiyum (➤ 99) or on the Nile in Aswan with "the Birdman of Aswan" Mohamed Arabi (tel: 012-324 0132; www.touregypt.net).

Desert driving with an experienced desert guide, such as Peter Gaballa (tel: 012-314 2388; www.egyptoffroad.com) or Hisham Nessim (tel: 012-780 7999; www.raid4x4egypt.com).

Diving in the Red Sea and around the Sinai peninsula (➤ 66–67).

Felucca sailing between Aswan and Luxor (➤ 72–73).

Fishing safaris on Lake Nasser by African Angler; tel: 097-231 0907; http://african-angler.net).

Hiking in the splendid St Catherine's Protectorate (must be done in the company of a Bedouin guide, arranged by EU-funded Sheikh Sina Treks (tel: 011-255 1150; www.sheikhsina.com).

Horse-back riding at the Pyramids in Giza at AA Stables (☎ 02-3385 0531) or on the West Bank in Luxor at Nobi's Stables (tel: 010-504 8558; www.luxorstables.com).

Swimming Most luxury hotels allow non-residents to use their pool for a fee, or snorkel in the Red Sea.

Windsurfing in the Red Sea, especially Moon Beach Resort, Ras Sudr (tel: 069-581 0088; www.moonbeachretreat.com).

Best markets

Al Muski in Cairo. Busy street market with toys, textiles, stationery, clothes and household goods, Mon–Sat.

Shari' al Suq, Aswan. Laid-back market full of spices, lovely baskets, silk shawls and stuffed baby crocodiles.

Souk al Gimal in Birqash, 30km (18 miles) northwest of Cairo, daily 6am–noon. Hundreds of camels from Sudan are sold, plus goats and saddles.

Souk al Gimal in Daraw. Sudanese traders sell their camels to local farmers in this colourful market (➤ 158).

Souq al Hamis in Al Arish, Sinai. Every Thursday from 9am, Bedouin from the surrounding Sinai Desert come to sell their wares, including beadwork, silver jewellery, embroidered dresses and carpets.

Spice Market in Cairo. You can smell it from afar, in the alley to the left of the Al Ashraf Barsbay Mosque on Shari' Mu'Izz li-Din Allah.

Tewfiqiya Market, Downtown, Cairo. Excellent food and vegetable market.

Stunning views

Take the elevator up the Cairo Tower (➤ 88) on a clear day for a bird's-eye view over one of the world's biggest cities.

Climb the path above Deir al Bahari (➤ 147) for views over the mortuary temples, fluorescent-green sugarcane fields and the Nile in Luxor.

Have Cairo's old city, with 1001 minarets at your feet, while enjoying lunch on the terrace of the Citadel View restaurant (➤ 59) at the Al Azhar Park (➤ 88).

The terrace of the Sofitel Old Cataract hotel, Aswan (➤ 166) has one of the most satisfying views in Egypt, over the Nile at its most beautiful, the Aga Khan Mausoleum and the desert on the West Bank, and the ancient ruins of Yebu.

Take a room in the Cecil hotel (➤ 133) with sweeping views over the Corniche in Alexandria.

See the sun rise over Sinai from the summit of Gebel Musa near St Catherine's Monastery (➤ 42–43).

Top diving and snorkelling sites

RED SEA COAST
Beit Goha (20km/12.5 miles north of Quseir).
Exceptional, very shallow, coral garden, still in great
condition, with sturgeon fish, grouper, trumpet fish
and many others.

Carless (Careless) Reef (5km/3 miles north of Giftun
Island). Famous for its semi-tame moray eels, but
untamed sharks and jacks can often be spotted.

Green Hole (59km/36 miles north of Quseir).
Magnificent coral growth, dolphins and blue-eagle
rays as well as the usual reef species.

Sirena Beach Home Reef (in front of Mövenpick
Hotel, Al Quseyr). Just off the jetty is a reef with a
huge variety of both corals and fish, including giant
schools of tuna, Napoleon and lion fish.

SINAI
Blue Hole (a few kilometres north of Dahab).
Pleasant, easy diving and snorkelling on the outer reef of the
Blue Hole lagoon, with mainly hard corals and a large variety
of reef fish.

The Canyon (on the way to the Blue Hole, Dahab). A long, narrow
and very beautiful canyon, with plenty to see even for
inexperienced divers.

End of the Road Reef (extreme end of Nabq coastal road, north
of Sharm el Sheikh). Submerged island with some of the best
corals in Egypt. Abundant fish life.

The Islands (near Laguna Hotel, Dahab). Spectacular labyrinth of coral peaks, bowls and corridors, teeming with fish and the occasional turtle.

Ras Ghozlani (Ras Muhammad). Nicest spot on the southern coast to observe the abundant small reef species and well-preserved corals.

Shark Observatory (Ras Muhammad). A vertical wall of soft and hard coral which attracts barracuda, grey and blacktip sharks and Napoleon fish.

Places to take the children

ARTS
Cairo Puppet Theatre
Great puppet theatre – in Arabic, but the show is exciting enough even if you don't understand.

✉ Azbakiya Gardens, Downtown ☎ 02-2591 0954 🕐 Thu 6:30–8:15pm, Fri, Sun 10:30–1

Fagnoon Art School
Artist Mohammed Allam runs this great art school near Saqqara, where kids can let their imagination run wild and work with materials such as wrought iron, clay, paint, woodwork etc.

✉ Saqqara Road, Sabil Om Hashim, 12km (7.5 miles) east of the Giza pyramids ☎ 010-158 6715/02-3815 1014 🕐 Daily 10–7

GLASS-BOTTOMED BOATS
Most resorts in Sinai and along the Red Sea offer daily trips in glass-bottomed boats, which allow visitors who are not so keen on diving the chance to explore the wonders of the Red Sea.

MUSEUMS
Al Mathaf al Masri (Egyptian Museum)
See pages 48–49.

Suzanne Murabak's Mathaf al Atfaal (Children's Museum)
Fascinating museum with interactive displays of Pharaonic Egypt, children's dress through the ages, and various halls about the desert and the Nile.

✉ 34 Shari' Bakr as Seddiq, Heliopolis ☎ 02-2642 4246 🕐 Daily 9–3:30 ✋ Inexpensive

THEME PARKS
Crazy Water
A fun theme park with a variety of water slides, a wave pool, a children's pool and a playground with sand, slides and tunnels.

✉ Next to 6th of October City, Alexandria–Cairo Desert Road ☎ 02-3781 4564
🕐 Daily 10–10 ✋ Moderate

Dream Park

Designed by Disneyworld Florida, this is Cairo's most advanced amusement park, with over 30 rides and a big food court.
✉ Oasis Road, 6th of October City ☎ 02-3855 3191; www.dreamparkegypt.com 🕐 Sat–Thu 10–7, Fri 12–7 ✋ Moderate

Dr Ragab's Pharaonic Village

A two-hour guided tour by boat, quite kitsch but fun, through the Canal of Mythology, taking in scenes of ancient Egyptian rural life, and ending at a temple with a sacred lake. There's also the possibility of dressing like a pharaoh and posing for a picture. There are several museums explaining ancient Egypt, a restaurant, a cafe and a small playground.
✉ Jacob's Island, Shari' al Bahr al Azam, Corniche, Giza, Cairo ☎ 02-3571 8675; www.pharaonicvillage.com 🕐 May–Oct daily 9–9; Nov–Apr 9–6
✋ Expensive

ZOOS & GARDENS
Cairo Zoological Gardens

Built in 1891, this was once one of the world's greatest zoos, but today it is struggling to survive. Kids are allowed to feed the animals so they love it.
✉ Midan al Gamaa, Giza ☎ 02-3570 8895 🕐 Daily 9–4 ✋ Inexpensive

Gineenat al Samak (Fish Garden)

About 200 displays of tropical fish set into several grottoes and a labyrinth of little alleys which are great fun for children to explore.
✉ Gabalaya Park, Shari' Umm Kulthum, Zamalik 🕐 Daily 10–5
✋ Inexpensive

Best souvenirs

Alabaster
Several alabaster factories on the West Bank in Luxor make pots, vases and small statues in a variety of shapes – look for the unpolished alabaster, in particular.

Belly-dancing outfits
Inexpensive belly-dancing outfits for adults and kids can be found at many stalls in Khan al Khalili (➤ 46–47), as well as professional, made-to-measure dresses for more serious dancers (➤ 112).

Egyptian music
Nothing will bring back the holiday more than a blast of Egyptian music, from the traditional 'oud (lute) recital to the swinging belly-dance music or songs by Egypt's most popular singer, Amr Diab.

Embroidery
Siwan women and Bedouin women cooperatives in Sinai produce traditional embroideries on clothes, bags, wall hangings and furnishings (➤ 113–114).

Hand-blown glass
The pharaohs had glasses very much like the ones still made today by Cairene glass-blowers, who now use recycled glass.

Pottery
Al Faiyum (➤ 99) has been famous for its pottery since ancient times and the tradition is continued today. The pottery can be bought in Cairo. Inexpensive terracotta pots that can be used to cook with are a good buy in Luxor and Aswan.

Silk weaving
Nagada, in upper Egypt, is famous for its traditionally woven silk-cotton textiles, while the souk in Aswan is filled with attractive so-called silk scarves in a multitude of colours.

Silver jewellery

Gold is plentiful in the country's gold markets, but the more interesting jewellery is made in silver, such as the traditional Bedouin trinkets (► 114) or the contemporary jewellery by Cairene designers (► 112–113).

Spices

Every market in Egypt has plenty of spices, but look for cumin, black pepper, chilli peppers and *karkadeh* (dried hibiscus flower), particularly in Aswan, which makes a great drink both hot and cold. Avoid Egyptian "saffron", which is overpriced and is not even the real thing.

Woven rugs

You can find colourful woven rugs with rural scenes all over Egypt, but the finest and most inspired are made at the Ramses Wissa Wassef arts centre (► 114), near the Giza Pyramids.

a boat trip around the islands

Rent a felucca from the docks near the Panorama Restaurant in Aswan. Late afternoon is best, when the air is cooler and the light is softer, in time to catch the sunset in all its majesty. Early morning is recommended if you want to visit the tombs on the way.

On the west bank are the Tombs of the Nobles (▶ 146; open 7–4; till 5 in summer), which belonged to the princes and priests of Elephantine. The finest are the tombs of Sirenput I and II, with colourful scenes of daily life. Higher up is the tomb of a local sheikh (saint) known as the Qubbat al Hawa (Dome of the Winds), with fantastic views of Aswan. Continue by felucca to the Botanical Gardens on Kitchener's Island (open 8–sunset), a lush island presented to the British general Lord Kitchener after his military successes in Sudan. Kitchener had the island planted with exotic plants and trees from all over the world.

Sailing around the back of the Elephantine Island, you should catch a glimpse of village life, including little children who sing Nubian songs from their tiny boats hoping for some *baksheesh* (tips). On the west bank beyond Elephantine, the Aga Khan Mausoleum (▶ 154) is also the stop for the 10th-century St Simeon's Monastery (open 7–5

in summer; 8–4 in winter), destroyed in 1173 by Saladin. The steep climb (30 mins) is rewarded by the spectacular setting of this roofless basilica. End by jumping off at the Sofitel Old Cataract hotel landing for an apéritif on the terrace.

FELUCCAS

Official prices for feluccas per person for every possible excursion, including waiting time, are available from the tourist office:

✉ Midan al Mahatta
☎ 097-231 2811

Distance 3km (2 miles)
Time 3–4 hours with stops
Start point Docks by EgyptAir office on the Corniche, Aswan
End point Sofitel Old Cataract hotel, Aswan
Break Food and water may not be provided on shorter trips

Best museums

Coptic Museum, Cairo
For a fascinating insight into the link between ancient Egypt and early Christianity (➤ 92–93).

Egyptian Museum, Cairo
No doubt the best museum of Egyptian antiquities in the country, if not the whole world (➤ 48–49).

Icon museum, St Catherine Monastery
One of the richest icon collections in the world (➤ 42–43), housed in the monastery's main church.

Museum of Islamic Art, Cairo
One of the world's greatest collections of Islamic art, mostly found in the old city of Cairo (➤ 90).

Luxor Museum, Luxor
A small collection of pharaonic masterpieces, but an astonishingly beautiful and well-laid out museum (➤ 144). Exhibits include some of the contents from Tutankhamun's tomb.

Mr and Mrs Mahmoud Khalil Museum, Cairo
Little visited, but precious small museum with an excellent collection of European masters (➤ 91).

Nubia Museum, Aswan
Egypt's tribute to the Nubian culture, which more or less disappeared under Lake Nasser (➤ 156). Exhibits ranging in date from prehistory to the present day are well-displayed and well-labelled.

Solar Boat Museum, Giza
A painstakingly restored pharaonic barque, found near the Pyramid of Khufu in Giza (➤ 100).

Exploring

Before the High Dam was built, the Nile used to flood every year, and for thousands of years the Egyptians depended on its water and the silt it left behind to farm. The Nile gave them everything and it was central to their lives and their beliefs. They saw the sun coming up on the east side of the Nile, so that was where they lived, and going down on the west bank, so that was where they buried their dead.

More than 5,000 years have passed, but things haven't changed much. Today most Egyptians still cling to the Nile, and government schemes to move people to agricultural projects in the desert have been only partly successful. Egypt has enough monuments to spend a lifetime exploring, but a visit will be enriched by meeting some of the country's inhabitants, with their great sense of survival, their capacity to laugh adversity in the face and their deep sense of humanity and hospitality.

Cairo and Environs

Legendary King Menes founded his capital Memphis on the exact spot where the Delta met the Nile Valley. The modern day suburb of Matariya was the important ancient religious centre of On, while the Romans set up camp in Babylon, now known as Coptic Cairo. The city of Al Qahira or the Victorious (Cairo) was founded in AD969 by the Fatimid Dynasty as a palace enclave. It soon grew into a great medieval city, enriched by the trade with the East and the West.

Al Qāhira
(Cairo)

Fatimid Cairo was centred around the Al Azhar Mosque, and enclosed within city walls which still exist in many parts. The city soon burst out of its walls, and it has not stopped growing yet. In the mid-19th century Ismail Pasha created the European-style quarters on a flood plain, which now form Downtown, and the city now spreads far into the desert on all sides.

CAIRO

Cairo (Al Qahira) can be a challenging place to visit for the first time. Nearly 21 million people, several thousand years of history and a mixture of cultural influences from Africa, Asia and Europe add up to a serious assault on the senses. Cairo somehow reconciles its extremes, however; great beauty with urban and industrial sprawl, affluence with poverty, the long shadow of the past with the promise of the future. Although it makes demands on its visitors (the traffic, pollution, hassles), its citizens make up for that by being some of the most hospitable and humorous people in the world.
✛ 6C

Amr Ibn al As Mosque

Amr, the Arab general who conquered Christian Egypt in AD641, established the city of Fustat here, near the Roman fortress of Babylon. Fustat, famous for its ceramics and glassware, was a wealthy and sophisticated city until the 12th century. In 1168 it was burned to avoid it falling to the Crusaders and it has remained a mound of rubble ever since.

Amr's Mosque, the first in Egypt, was later restored and underwent many more renovations, the last being in the 1970s. Look for the old features, particularly columns reused from churches and temples. In the far left corner lies Amr's son, Abdallah. Originally buried inside his house, his tomb was incorporated into the mosque during the ninth century.

✛ Cairo 3g ✉ Shari' Sidi Hassan al Anwar, 500m (550yds) north of Mari Girgis, Masr Qadima, Coptic Cairo ⏰ Daily 9–4 (closed 12–1 Fri) 💷 Free; tip expected for the guard 🚇 Mar Girgis

Al Azhar Mosque and University

Al Azhar ("the most blooming"), founded in
AD971, was the first mosque in the Fatimid city,
and claims to be the oldest university in the
world. As Egypt's supreme theological authority,
the Sheikh of al Azhar plays a significant role in
national politics. The mosque is entered through
the remarkable 18th-century Barber's Gate, where
students traditionally had their heads shaved.
Beyond is a large *sahn* or courtyard, part of the
original 10th-century design, overlooked by three
minarets. To the right is a Mameluke *madrasa*
(Quranic school), with apartments for Quranic
students. The oldest part of the building is the
east *liwan* (hall), in which many ancient alabaster
pillars were reused. The university now occupies
several large modern blocks behind the mosque.

➕ *Cairo 5d* ✉ Shari' al Azhar, Midan al Husayn
🕓 24 hours, but closed at prayer times ✋ Free, but tip
requested by the guards ❓ Dress modestly, cover arms
and legs

Bab Zuwayla and Other City Gates

Bab Zuwayla, built in 1092 and also known as Bab
al Mitwalli, was the southern gate of the Fatimid
city. From the terrace between its imposing twin
towers, Mameluke sultans watched the departure
of the annual caravan of pilgrims to Mecca. A
small museum inside the beautifully restored
gatehouse illustrates the history of the gate and
also explains about the 19th-century saint Mitwalli
al Qutb who performed miracles here. Adjacent to
the gates is the 15th-century Al Muayyad Mosque
with a tree-shaded courtyard. On the northern side

of the Fatimid city are the Bab al Futuh (Gate of Conquests) and Bab al Nasir (Gate of Victory), joined by a 200m-long (655ft) tunnel with fine brickwork, still under restoration.

Next to Bab al Futuh is the 11th-century mosque of the strange blue-eyed Fatimid Caliph, Al Hakim. As he loved night-time, he decreed that this would be the time for work while the days were for sleeping. He hated women so much they were not allowed to go out and women's cobblers were closed down. He also had all Cairo's dogs killed for making too much noise. After his death, the Druze (a heretical Muslim sect) was founded, and proclaimed that Al Hakim would return as the Messiah.

✠ *Cairo 5d and 6c* ✉ Bab Zuwayla is in Darb al Ahmar. Bab al Futuh and Bab al Nasir are on the other end of Shari' al Mu'Izz li-Din Allah
🖐 Inexpensive

a walk between two city gates

*Start at the stunning southern city gate of Bab Zuwayla
(▶ 82–83) and walk northwards along Shari' al Mu'Izz
li-Din Allah, one of the city's main thoroughfares, lined
with newly restored mosques and palaces.*

Find the small entrance on the inside of the Bab Zuwayla
Gate and climb up the minaret for spectacular views over
the city.

*Back on the street, turn left and continue past a little
square where cotton is sold, with the 19th-century Sabil
of Muhammad Ali. A hundred metres (110 yards) on*

stands the ruined 12th-century Fakahani Mosque. Fifty
metres (55yds) further, on the left, is the city's last
tarboush (fez) shop.

Just before the intersection with Shari' al Azhar is the
Ghuriya complex, with the splendid 16th-century Mosque-
Madrasa of al Ghuri (on the left) and the Mausoleum of al
Ghuri and the al Ghuri Palace (on the right). This part of the
street is now covered with a wooden roof.

Cross Shari' al Azhar via the walking bridge and continue
along the more touristy end of Shari' al Mu'lzz.

After the intersection with Shari' al Muski, the street is
pedestrian only and turns into the Gold Bazaar and further
on into the Coppersmiths' Bazaar. Past this to the right is
the Madrasa of Sultan Ayyub and to the left the superb
Qalawun, al Nasir and Barquq Complex (► 94–95).
Opposite the mosque complex, in the Mohammed Ali
Sabil, is the Textile Museum (► 92) with superb textiles
from the pharaonic, Coptic and Islamic eras.

With Qasr Bashtak on the right, take the left-hand fork at
the lovely drinking fountain Sabil-Kuttab of Katkhuda.
One block past the 12th-century Mosque of al Aqmar,
70m (75yds) further to the right, turn right into Darb al
Asfar for Bayt al Suhaymi (► 86). Return to the main
street and turn right, past the Al Silahdar Mosque.
Continue through the lemon and garlic market to the
Mosque of al Hakim (► 83), built against the Northern
Walls and the Bab al Futuh (► 83).

Distance 1.5km (1 mile)
Time Half an hour without stops, at least half a day with stops
Start point Bab Zuwayla ✚ Cairo 5d
End point Bab al Futuh ✚ Cairo 6c

Bayt al Kritiliya (Gayer-Anderson House)

The Gayer-Anderson House, two adjoining 16th- and 17th-century mansions, is an orientalist's dream. British major R J Gayer-Anderson, an army doctor, lived here from 1935 to 1942 and collected ancient Egyptian and Oriental art. The spacious *qa'a* (men's reception room) appeared in the 1977 James Bond film *The Spy Who Loved Me*, and is one of the finest such rooms in Cairo. The *harem* (women's and children's quarters) includes a succession of finely decorated rooms, a roof terrace to take the air and secret windows which allowed the women to look onto the *qa'a* without being seen. The house has been beautifully restored and the small collections are well displayed.

➕ *Cairo 4f* ✉ 4 Midan Ahmed Ibn Tulun, Al Sayyida Zaynab ☎ 02-364 7822 🕐 Daily 9–5 💵 Moderate 🚌 174 from Midan Ramses; minibus No 54 from bus station behind the Egyptian Museum

Bayt al Suhaymi

This remarkable 16th- and 17th-century house, which belonged to

a wealthy merchant and his many wives and concubines, is a labyrinth of rooms for the men followed by rooms for the *harem* (women and children). They are all beautifully decorated and naturally air-conditioned, centred around a cool, peaceful courtyard where it is pleasant to linger for a while.

➕ *Cairo 5c* ✉ 19 Darb al Asfar, Al Gamaliya 🕐 Daily 9–5 💵 Inexpensive

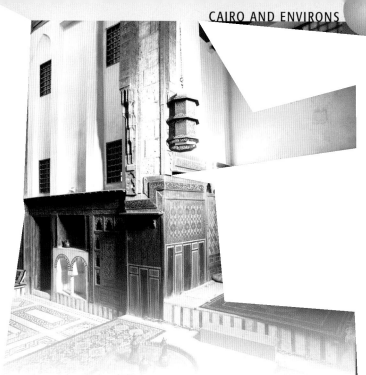

Ben Ezra Synagogue

The Ben Ezra Synagogue is the oldest synagogue in Egypt. Formerly the fourth-century Church of St Michael, it is built in basilica style with three naves and a hidden altar, and the intricate decoration is not unlike that of the nearby churches. Copts believe that this was where Moses was found in a basket, while Jews claim that Jeremiah preached here in the sixth century. Services are no longer held.

✚ *Cairo 3h* ✉ Mar Girgis, Coptic Cairo
🕐 Daily 8–4 💲 Free, donations welcome
🚇 Mar Girgis

Gezira

Gezira, the largest island on the Nile in Cairo, is crossed by three bridges. The exclusive residential area Zamalik, on the northern side, has many upmarket shops and restaurants and is home to the Gezira Sporting Club, founded in 1877 by the British Army. Near the Marriott Hotel, a former palace, is the Gezira Centre of Arts with a museum of Islamic Ceramics (► 90). The landmarks on the Gezira (southern) end are the Cairo Tower and the Opera House. The 187m-high (613ft) Cairo Tower (► 64), built in the late 1950s, has a revolving restaurant and, on a clear day, sweeping views over Cairo to the desert. The Opera House (► 116), a gift from Japan, was built in 1988 to replace the one that burned down in 1971. In its grounds is the Museum of Egyptian Modern Art and several art galleries.

🕂 *Cairo 2c* ✉ Gezira Island ☎ Opera House 02-2739 8144; Modern Art Museum 02-2736 6665 🕓 Cairo Tower daily 8am–midnight; Modern Art Museum Tue–Sun 10–2, 5:30–10 💵 Cairo Tower expensive, museums inexpensive
🍴 Cafe/restaurant on top of Cairo Tower (££) 🚇 Gezira 🚌 Minibus 54

Guinenat al Azhar

A few years ago the Aga Khan Trust for Culture landscaped an area outside the city walls where centuries of rubbish had piled up. The result, Al Azhar Park, is a godsend in Cairo, both for its vast and beautiful gardens where local families come for a stroll, and for the magnificent views over the minarets and rooftops of the Islamic

part of Cairo. The Citadel View restaurant (➤ 58, 106) is a showcase for good contemporary Islamic architecture.

🏛 *Cairo 5e* ✉ Shari' Salah Salem ☎ 02-2510 7378; www.alazharpark.com 🕐 9am–midnight 💷 Inexpensive

Ibn Tulun Mosque

Built by Ahmed Ibn Tulun in AD876–9, this mosque is a rare example of the classical period in Islamic architecture (9th to 10th centuries). The peaceful courtyard was built as a vast, open-air prayer hall – this was the city's central mosque and is now its oldest intact Islamic monument. The 2km-long (1.2-mile) wooden frieze is said to contain one-fifth of the Koran in Kufic inscriptions. The unusual minaret with an outside spiral staircase was inspired by the architecture of Samarra in Iraq, where Tulun grew up, although local lore has it that the sultan absent-mindedly rolled up a piece of paper and handed it to the architect as the design.

🏛 *Cairo 4f* ✉ Midan Ahmed Ibn Tulun 🕐 Daily 8–6 💷 Free, tip requested

Khan al Khalili

Best places to see, ➤ 46–47.

Al Mathaf al Islami (Museum of Islamic Art)

This rare and extensive collection of Islamic arts holds the key to understanding the architecture of Islamic Cairo. Seeing the appalling state of many Cairene mosques and palaces, Khedive Tewfiq founded a museum of Islamic art in 1880 to salvage parts of derelict buildings.

The museum reopened in 2010 after extensive renovations, and it is now the largest museum of Islamic art in the world, with more than 2,500 exhibits chosen from a collection of over 100,000 objects.

The first wing is ordered chronologically and is dedicated to objects from Egypt, while the second wing has artefacts from other Islamic nations. Sunni Muslims consider the representation of human and animal figures as idolatry, so there are no statues in the museum and most of the designs are based on floral motifs, geometric patterns and Arabic calligraphy. The exception to this rule was the art of the Shi'a Fatimids, who allowed birds, animals and scenes from daily life in the decoration of their objects. Among the masterpieces are a gold-inlaid key to the Kaaba.

➕ *Cairo 5d* ✉ Shari' Bur Sa'id on intersection with Shari' al Qal'a
☎ 02-390 1520 🕐 Daily 9–4 💷 Moderate

Mathaf al Khazaf al Islami (Islamic Ceramics Museum)

The domed palace of Prince Amr Ibrahim, a neo-Islamic, 20th-century building, houses the Islamic Ceramics Museum, with a wonderful range of ceramics from all over the Islamic world, put together from the collections of the Egyptian royal family, Prince Amr Ibrahim and the Museum of Islamic Art (see above). The well-displayed collection has several rare pieces, including a precious 17th-century porcelain plate from Andalucia and a very fine 16th-century Turkish *mishkaa* or hanging lamp.

➕ *Cairo 2c* ✉ Gezira Art Centre, 1 Shari' al Marsafy, Zamalik ☎ 02-2737 3298 🕐 Sat–Thu 10–1:30, 5:30–8 💷 Inexpensive ❓ Complex includes several art galleries and an open-air theatre

Mathaf Mahmoud Khalil (Mr and Mrs Mahmoud Khalil Museum)

The splendid little Mr and Mrs Mahmoud Khalil Museum is home to a superb collection of original French Impressionist paintings and fine sculpture, which comes as something of a surprise to tourists, very few of whom visit the place. Little-known paintings by the likes of Renoir, Monet, Van Gogh, Pissarro, Gauguin and Ingres, sculptures by artists such as Rodin, as well as Chinese porcelain and jade, were lovingly gathered by Mahmoud Khalil, a pre-World War II agricultural minister, and his French wife. They bequeathed their collection to the state on the condition that it would be displayed in their own Italianate villa and the air-conditioned rooms offer welcome relief on a hot summer's day.

✚ *Cairo 2e* ✉ 1 Shari' Kafour, Doqqi, next to the Maglis al Dawla (State Council) ☎ 02-3338 9720 🕓 Tue–Sun 10–5 👋 Inexpensive

❓ You need your passport to enter the museum

Al Mathaf al Masri (Egyptian Museum)

Best places to see, ➤ 48–49.

Al Mathaf al Naseej (Textile Museum)

The first Egyptian textile museum opened its doors in early 2010, in the renovated Sabil (water fountain) of Mohamed Ali, built 1829. The museum starts with an impressive collection of pharaonic linen, clothing and bed linen, even a baby nappy (diaper) in its own bag from 1500BC. The Copts continued the pharaonic tradition of weaving and were true masters. They also continued the tradition of wrapping their dead in textiles, some of which are on show here. In medieval times Egyptian linen was the finest in the world; now Egyptian cotton has a similar reputation. The Islamic textiles are equally exquisite, and brilliantly displayed.

✚ *Cairo 5d* ✉ Sabil Mohamed Ali, Souk an-Nahassin, Shari' Mu'Izz li-Din Allah, opposite Qalawun Mosque ☎ No phone ◷ Daily 9–5 ✋ Inexpensive

Al Mathaf al Qibti (Coptic Museum)

The Coptic Museum, occupying an area of 8,000sq m (86,000 sq feet), has been thoroughly renovated in recent years, and it presents a valuable collection of secular and religious Coptic artefacts, from AD200 to 1800. The wonderful collection shows fascinating evidence of an ancient Egyptian influence on early Christianity. The Christian funerary stelae (second to fifth century) from Kom Abu Billou illustrate the transition from religious Pharaonic art to Coptic art, one clear change being from the pharaonic ankh (the "key of life" looped cross) to the Christian cross. Note also the wonderful frescoes from the sixth-century Al Bawit monastery and the earliest recorded stone pulpit from the sixth-century St Jeremiah monastery in Saqqara.

Room 10 claims to have the oldest surviving book in the world, a 1,600-year-old copy of the

Psalms of David. Some magnificent Coptic textiles are on display on the upper floor. The Old Wing, remarkable in itself for the fine woodwork and ceiling carvings, houses some interesting pottery and artefacts from Coptic churches. The towers and walls in the garden were built by Roman Emperor Trajan around AD130 as part of Babylon.

www.coptic-cairo.com

✠ *Cairo 3h* ✉ Shari' Mar Girgis, Masr Qadima ☎ 02-2363 9742 🕓 Daily 9–5 ✋ Moderate 🍴 Cafe in the garden (£) 🚇 Mar Girgis

Al Muallaqa (Hanging Church)

The Hanging Church, built over a Roman Gate, is reached via an impressive stairway, which leads to a vestibule where videos of

papal sermons and wonderfully kitsch Coptic shrines are on sale. Copts believe that this church was founded in the 4th century, but it could date to at least 300 years after that. The main nave, with a ceiling vaulted like an ark, is separated from the aisles by 16 pillars that probably carried images of saints. The altar areas are hidden by finely carved wooden screens inlaid with ivory and the marble pulpit is supported by 12 pillars, one for each of the apostles.

✠ *Cairo 3h* ✉ Shari' Mar Girgis, Masr Qadima 🕓 Mon–Sat 9–5, Sun 12–5 ✋ Free; donations welcome. Well-informed Coptic students often guide visitors around 🚇 Mar Girgis

Al Qal'a (Citadel)

Realizing the difficulty of protecting Cairo, Salah al Din al Ayyubi (Saladin) built the Citadel in the 12th century. Its design was strongly influenced by Crusader castles in Palestine and Syria. The most obvious building, seen from many parts of Cairo, is the 19th-century Mosque of Muhammad Ali, inspired by grand Ottoman mosques in Istanbul. It is most impressive from a distance, as inside, despite the soaring dome, the lack of proportion and the overdone decor disappoint. The courtyard clock was a gift from King Louis-Philippe of France, in exchange for the Luxor obelisk now in the Place de la Concorde, Paris. Next door is the 14th-century Mosque of al Nasir, and the Gawhara Palace, the former

royal quarters, built in a French style. In the enclosure are the quirky Police Museum that illustrates famous murders and crimes in Egypt, and the Carriage Museum, with its dusty 19th-century carriages.
✚ *Cairo 5f* ✉ Entrance at Bab al Gabal, on the Shari' Salah Salem ☎ 02-2512 1735
🕐 May–Sep daily 8–6, Oct–Apr 8–5. Museums 8:30–4:30 🖐 Moderate 🍴 Cafe (£) 🚌 Bus 54

Qalawun, al Nasir and Barquq Complex

The splendid 185m-long (607ft) facade of this Mameluke complex is one of Cairo's most wonderful sights. Coming from Al Azhar, the first building is Qalawun's *maristan* (hospital and madhouse), built in 1285 and used as such until 1850. Next door is the beautifully restored and richly decorated mausoleum of Sultan Qalawun, and behind it a *madrasa* (Koranic school). His son Al Nasir Muhammad, who is buried in this mausoleum, followed his father's plan and in 1304 built a mosque, a *madrasa* and mausoleum next door.

Barquq, the first Circassian Mameluke sultan, added his share to it and in 1386 built a fine *khanqah* (religious hostel) and a magnificent *madrasa* behind heavy bronze-plated doors with silver inlay.

✚ *Cairo 5d* ✉ Bayn al Qasrayn, Shari' al Mu'Izz li-Din Allah ⏰ Daily 8–5
✋ Free, but tip expected

Qasr Abdin (Abdin Palace Museum)

Khedive Ismail built this 500-room palace as part of the redevelopment of Cairo to accompany the opening of the Suez Canal in 1869. Four years later he moved the royal family here from the Citadel, and they lived here until the revolution in 1952 (fulfilling a prophecy that the dynasty would only survive if it stayed in the Citadel). The main palace is closed to the public, but in a separate building there are displays of weaponry and suits of armour, as well as part of the former royal family's impressive collection of silver, china and crystal. The medal museum contains King Farouk's amusing collection of badges.

✚ *Cairo 4e* ✉ Midan Abdin, Downtown ☎ 02-2391 0042 ⏰ Sat–Thu
9–2:45 ✋ Inexpensive 🚇 Mohamed Naguib ❓ No cameras

Qaytbay Mausoleum-Madrasa

The grandest building in the Northern
Cemetery belonged to the last powerful
Mameluke ruler, Sultan Qaytbay, who
reigned from 1468 to 1496. This jewel of
late Mameluke architecture is perfect in
many ways, with faultless proportions, fine
carving around the doors and windows,
and an elegant minaret. Although the
decoration of the *madrasa* (Koranic school)
is amazingly rich, the overall effect is one
of simplicity and harmony, using the
primary Islamic designs: calligraphy,
arabesque and geometric patterns. The
tomb chamber, one of the most
impressive in Cairo, is covered by a
magnificent huge dome.

✚ Cairo 6d ✉ Al Qarafa al Sharqiya (Northern
Cemetery), Al Dirasa ⏰ Daily 9–5 ✋ Free, but
tip expected 🚌 Minibus No 77

Sayyidna al Husayn Mosque

One of Cairo's most sacred mosques is
dedicated to the Prophet Muhammad's
grandson Husayn, who was killed in
680 in Iraq. Although it has been disputed
that his head is buried here, Husayn is
revered as the city's patron saint and his
mosque attracts Muslims from around the
world, particularly during the annual
moulid (birthday celebration). Cairenes
believe the whole area, including the
cafes, around the mosque has a special
baraka (blessing).

✚ *Cairo 5d* ✉ Midan al Husayn 👆 Free ❓ Closed to non-Muslims. *The place to be, or to avoid if you dislike crowds, during major Muslim festivals*

Sultan Hasan Mosque-Madrasa

Best places to see, ➤ 54–55.

Wikalat al Ghuri

This restored Mameluke caravanserai (merchants' inn) is an oasis of cool and calm amid the hubbub of the bazaars. It now provides workshops for craftsmen and studios for painters, some of which can be visited. Part of the same al Ghuri complex is the splendid Mausoleum of the Mameluke Sultan al Ghuri on Shari' al Azhar, and his beautifully restored mosque. Al Ghuri died in Syria, but his body was never brought back, so the tomb here contains the body of his successor.

✚ *Cairo 5d* ✉ Off Shari' al Mu'izz li-din Allah, near Al Azhar Mosque
🕐 Sat–Thu 9–5 👆 Inexpensive. Mosque free, but tip expected

Wust al Balad (Downtown)

The reconstruction of central Cairo was another of Khedive Ismail's extravagant projects for the inauguration of the Suez Canal in 1869. Impressed with Paris' boulevards, he built elegant avenues

like Talaat Harb and Qasr al Nil. Nowadays the streets are congested and many buildings have been demolished, but a walk Downtown still has its rewards, particularly when you look up at the grand 19th-century colonial-style buildings. Midan al Tahrir, Cairo's main square, and the Nile Hilton complex were created after the 1952 revolution on the site of the British barracks.

✚ *Cairo 3d* 🕐 Most shops are closed Sun
🍴 Cafes and restaurants (£–£££) 🚇 Sadat

Around Cairo

AL AHRAM AND ABU'L HOL (PYRAMIDS AND SPHINX)
Best places to see, ➤ 38–39.

DAHSHUR
Wealthy Cairenes choose the quiet countryside of Dahshur to build their weekend retreats, but it also has two impressive Old Kingdom pyramids, both built by Snefru (c2613–1588BC), the father of Khufu, which give an insight into the evolution of pyramid building. The imposing Bent Pyramid, its shiny white limestone casing intact in places, is unlike any other pyramid. It rises more steeply than the pyramid of Khufu but suddenly changes to a gentler angle near the top.

The Red Pyramid, its sides built at a 43-degree angle, is considered the first "true" pyramid.

✚ 6D ✉ 5km (3 miles) south of Saqqara 🕐 May–Sep daily 8–5; Oct–Apr 8–4 ✋ Inexpensive

AL FAIYUM

Faiyum is surrounded by desert but is not a real oasis as it is connected to the Nile via the Bahr Yusuf. Al Faiyum town is a dull provincial centre, most famous for its waterwheels, particularly the Seven Waterwheels north of town. Its main attractions lie in its environs, especially Birket Qarun, a salt lake which attracts Cairenes for a rowing session and hunters looking for duck and geese. The waterfalls and freshwater lakes of Wadi Rayan, near the village of Tunes, are an ideal place to swim and watch birds. There are several ancient sites in the area, including the well-preserved Ptolemaic temple of Qasr Qarun, the ruins of a Ptolemaic-Roman town at Kom Aushim (just off the Cairo road) and the Pyramid of Meidoum.

✚ 6D ✉ 100km (62 miles) southwest of Cairo 🍴 Cafe (£–££) and restaurant on the lake (££) 🚌 Frequent buses from Cairo from Ahmed Helmy station behind Ramses train station

ℹ Midan Qarun, next to the waterwheels; tel: 084-634 2313

MATHAF MARKIB AL SHAMS (SOLAR BOAT MUSEUM)

Five boat pits were discovered at the foot of the Great Pyramid of Khufu (➤ 38) and the 43m-long (141ft) boat in the Solar Boat Museum was found in one of them. The boat, made of cedarwood, was in thousands of pieces, which took restorer Hagg Ahmed Yusuf 14 years to reconstruct. The result was worth it, for this simple boat is one of the most attractive of all Egyptian antiquities. Another boat, discovered in perfect condition in 1987, was left buried in the sand.

➕ 6C ✉ Giza Plateau, 18km (11 miles) southwest of Cairo ⏰ May–Sep daily 9–5; Oct–Apr 9–4 ✋ Moderate 🚌 Minibus from bus station near Ramses Hilton

MEMPHIS

Little remains of the world's first imperial capital beyond a few statues and columns. King Menes is said to have united Egypt's southern valley and northern delta around 3100BC and then created a new capital at Memphis. Memphis became a magnificent city and for thousands of years was either Egypt's capital or second city. Most buildings were constructed using mudbrick and have long since disappeared. The stone-built ones fared no better as they were quarried over the centuries to provide materials for monuments elsewhere. A small New Kingdom sphinx and a limestone colossus of Ramses II as a young man are on show in a modern pavilion in the open-air museum.

➕ 6C ✉ Mit Rahina, 24km (15 miles) south of Cairo ⏰ May–Sep daily 8–5; Oct–Apr 8–4 ✋ Moderate ❓ Public transport is difficult and it may

be best to book a day trip to Memphis and Saqqara through a travel agent

MISR AL GADIDA (HELIOPOLIS)

The city of the sun (On), which the Greeks called Heliopolis, was one of ancient Egypt's most important cult centres dedicated to the sun god Ra. Little has survived beyond an obelisk raised by Pharaoh Senusert I, in nearby Matariya, but the modern suburb of Heliopolis is now a booming district.

It was planned at the end of the 19th century by Belgian-born Baron Empain as a garden city. Empain's eccentric villa, built like a Cambodian temple, is now empty, but many grand villas and Moorish-style buildings along the elegant avenues are occupied, a testament to his vision. Among them, the former Heliopolis Palace Hotel is now the official presidency.

✚ Cairo 6a (off map) ✉ 5km (3 miles) north of centre of Cairo

🍴 Restaurants (£–£££)

🚇 Saray al Qubba

SAQQARA

Saqqara, the necropolis of the city of Memphis, is one of the largest (7km/4 miles long and 1.5km/1 mile wide) and most important cemeteries in Egypt, where much remains unexcavated. The Old Kingdom royal family and nobles were buried here, and the cemetery was in use for more than 3,000 years. Next to the ticket office is the Imhotep Museum, with displays of finds in the Saqqara area, particularly the blue-green faience found in King Djoser's burial chamber, a collection of large Old Kingdom alabaster jars, and a beautiful painted mummy found during excavations around the Teti Pyramid. The Step Pyramid of King Djoser, part of the largest funerary complex in Saqqara, was built by architect Imhotep in the 27th century BC. It was both the first pyramid in Egypt and at that time the largest monument in the

world built of hewn stone. The genius of Imhotep, who was later deified for his efforts, was that he started building a traditional *mastaba* (structure above tombs) not in mudbrick but in stone, and then added several more to create the six-step pyramid.

Visitors enter the funerary complex from the rebuilt southeastern gate which leads to a Hypostyle Hall, and further on to the Great South Court. On the northern side of the pyramid stands the *serdab*, a box containing a replica of Djoser's life-size statue staring towards his immortality. Further northeast are two sixth-Dynasty *mastaba*s of the Viziers Mereruka and Kagemni with fine reliefs. Next door, the *mastaba* of Ankh-ma-hor has particularly fine reliefs of craftsmen, and further west the *mastaba* of the Royal Hairdresser Ti has scenes from children's games. Walking back from the Serapeum towards the Step Pyramid, look for the *mastaba* of Akhti-Hotep and Ptah-Hotep, which shows the various stages of the decoration of a tomb.

South of Djoser's complex, the Pyramid of Unas contains a passageway leading to the burial chamber whose walls are decorated with the Pyramid texts, which are the earliest known example of decorative writing in a pharaonic tomb. The well-preserved *mastaba* of Queen Nebet, Unas' wife, has beautiful wall-paintings of the queen in the *harem* rooms of the palace, while the *mastaba* of Princess Idout gives an insight into the daily life of an Egyptian princess.

✚ 6D ✉ 2km (1.2 miles) west of Memphis ⏰ May–Sep daily 9–4; Oct–Apr 8–4 💰 Moderate 🍽 Cafe at Imhotep Museum 🚌 Public transport is very complicated so it is best to rent a car for the day ❓ The Step Pyramid can only be entered by special permit from the Egyptian Antiquities Inspectorate

HOTELS

CAIRO

Carlton (£)

This 1950s very central hotel has changed little over the years and it is a great one for those who like faded grandeur. Rooms vary in size and quality, so check first. Good value.

✉ 21 Shari' 26 July, Downtown ☎ 02-2575 5022; www.carltonhotelcairo.com

Four Seasons Nile Plaza (£££)

If you are looking for luxury and top service this is the place to stay, with large rooms overlooking the Nile or the city, and some excellent restaurants, a spa and an upmarket shopping centre.

✉ 1089 Corniche al Nil, Garden City ☎ 02-2791 7000; www.fourseasons.com/caironp

Hotel Osiris (£)

Here you will find spotless rooms with great views over the city, comfortable bedding and a very friendly service. A delicious breakfast is served on a terrace.

✉ 12th floor, Shari' Nubar, Downtown ☎ 02-2794 5728; http://hotelosiris.free.fr

Lialy Hostel (£)

The Lialy, a popular backpackers' haunt, has very clean and spacious rooms on this busy but very central square. The staff is very friendly and helpful, and there is an internet cafe attached.

✉ 3rd floor, Shari' Midan Tal'At Harb, Downtown ☎ 02-2575 2802; www.lialyhostel.com

Longchamps (££)

Very quiet hotel in residential area, often booked in advance by regular visitors who like its friendly, comfortable atmosphere. Some rooms have a private balcony, but guests gather for a sunset drink on the rear terrace.

✉ 5th floor, 21 Shari' Ism'll Muhammad, Zamalik ☎ 02-2735 2311; www.hotellongchamps.com

Mayfair (£)

Small quiet hotel in a tree-lined street with spotless rooms, some with a balcony overlooking the street. Tranquil terrace for having an afternoon drink.

✉ 9 Shari' Aziz Osman, Zamalik ☎ 02-2735 7315; www.mayfaircairo.com

Meramees (£)

Small but very popular budget hotel in the centre of Cairo owned by the extremely friendly Mamdouh Mohammed, who knows a lot about Cairo. Spotless and comfortable rooms and dormitories.

✉ 32 Shari' Sabry Abu Alam, Downtown ☎ 02-2396 2518

Pension Roma (£)

An old-style 1940s hotel with clean rooms, polished wooden floors and nice old furniture. Very popular, so it is advisable to book ahead.

✉ 6th floor, 169 Shari' Muhamad Farid ☎ 02-2381 1088; www.pensionroma.com.eg

Le Riad (£££)

Wake up to the sound of the muezzin calling for prayer and feel at home in this remarkable boutique hotel installed right in the middle of the souks and the old city. A first in Cairo!

✉ 114 Shari' Mu'Izz li-Din Allah, Islamic Cairo ☎ 02-2787 6074; www.leriad-hoteldecharme.com

Semiramis InterContinental (£££)

Centrally located Semiramis has five-star amenities and spacious rooms, most with great views over the Nile. The excellent restaurants include the French restaurant Sabaya (➤ 109) and Bird Cage (➤ 107).

✉ Corniche al Nil, Downtown ☎ 02-795 7171; www.ichotelsgroup.com/intercontinental

Sofitel Gezirah (£££)

Rooms in this circular tower, on the tip of a central island on the Nile, command great views over the river and city. Breakfast is

served on the terrace, and there are great Nile-side restaurants.
✉ 3 Shari' Al Thawra Council, Gezira ☎ 02-2737 3737; www.sofitel.com

Talisman (££)

A charming boutique hotel in a quiet alleyway, right in the heart of
Downtown, with beautifully decorated rooms.
✉ 5th floor, 39 Shari' Tal'At Harb, Downtown ☎ 02-2393 9431;
www.talisman-hotel.com

Villa Belle Epoque (£££)

This 13-room hotel in the leafy residential quarter of Maadi is only
15 minutes from Downtown by metro. The quiet villa is sumptuous
with a swimming pool and fruit and vegetable garden, the produce
of which is served in the restaurant (► 110).
✉ Road 13, Villa 63, Maadi ☎ 02-2358 0265; www.villabelleepoque.com

Windsor (£–££)

Well-run budget hotel in a Moorish-style building with spacious
rooms, arched windows and high ceilings, although it has seen
better days. Delightful colonial-style bar on the first floor, totally
musty and old-fashioned. Rooms near the road can be particularly
noisy so ask to see your room first.
✉ 19 Shari' al Alfi, Downtown ☎ 02-2591 5277; www.windsorcairo.com

RESTAURANTS

Abu al Sid (££–£££)

Egyptian restaurant in an old building with traditional furniture and
local art. Traditional dishes are served with style and optional water
pipes. Incredibly busy and trendy, so book in advance.
✉ 157 Shari' 26 July, Zamalik ☎ 02-2735 9640 🕙 Noon–2am

After Eight (££)

Not easy to find down a small alley, but worth looking for,
particularly at night when there is live jazz. The menu includes
simple Western and well-prepared Middle Eastern specialities.
✉ 6 Shari' Qasr al Nil ☎ 02-574 0855; www.after8cairo.com
🕙 Lunch, dinner

Andrea (£–££)

Delightful garden restaurant, with an indoor room for the evenings and cold days. Excellent roasted chicken and grills with Oriental salads and freshly baked *baladi* bread. Children's play area.

✉ 59–60 Marioutiya Canal, Al Ahram, Giza ☎ 02-3383 0938 🕐 10am–1am

Bird Cage (££–£££)

Thai restaurant serving well-prepared and beautifully presented dishes including deep-fried prawns in *konafa* (angel hair) and delicious spicy curries. The service is swift and ambience pleasant.

✉ Semiramis InterContinental, Corniche al Nil, Garden City ☎ 02-2795 7171 🕐 Noon–1am

La Bodega (££–£££)

Trendy bistro with Mediterranean specialities from Algerian couscous to ravioli and all between. The lounge, with minimal Asian decor, is more upmarket, serving good fusion dishes.

✉ Baehler's Mansions, 157 Shari' 26 July, Zamalik ☎ 02-2735 6761 🕐 Noon–2am

Café Riche (£–££)

This cafe-restaurant is apparently where Gamal Abdel Nasser planned the revolution, and was for a long time the meeting place of Cairo's intellectuals. It's a nice place to have a bite to eat with a coffee or glass of wine – stick to soups, salads and sandwiches.

✉ 17 Shari' Tal'At Harb, Downtown ☎ 02-2392 9793 🕐 9am–1am

Cilantro (£–££)

Stylish cafe that serves good coffee with fresh croissants for breakfast, healthy sandwiches and delicious fresh juices.

✉ 31 Shari' Mohammed Mahmoud, opposite AUC, Downtown ☎ 02-2792 4571 🕐 9am–2am

Citadel View (££)

The name says it all: the views over the whole city are spectacular, and the Egyptian food is good, varied and plentiful.

✉ Al-Azhar Park, Shari' Salah Salem ☎ 02-2510 9151 🕐 10am–2am

Egyptian Pancake House (£)
Delicious sweet and savoury *fateers*, a cross between a pancake and a pizza.

✉ Between Shari' al Azhar and Midan al Husayn, Khan al Khalili
🕐 24-hour

Et Tabei al Dumyati (£)
One of the cheapest and, perhaps. most authentic places to eat in Downtown, with a selection of tasty *mezze* and classic Egyptian dishes.

✉ 31 Shari' Orabi, Downtown ☎ 02-2575 4211 🕐 7am–1am

Fish Market (££)
A spacious boat moored on the Nile where you can choose your fresh fish or seafood from the display, then tell the chef how you would like it cooked. Salads are equally well prepared and be sure to try a dessert from the trolley.

✉ Americana Boat, 26 Shari' al Nil, Giza ☎ 02-3570 9693 🕐 Noon–2am

Al Fishawi (£)
The oldest tea house in Cairo, claiming never to have closed since 1773. A great place to sip tea, smoke a waterpipe and watch the world go by. No alcohol.

✉ Just off Midan al Husayn, Khan al Khalili 🕐 24 hours

Greek Club (£–££)
The old Greek club, with lots of faded grandeur and a large breezy terrace, is the perfect place for cool beer on a sweltering hot Cairene night. The food is nothing special, but it is edible.

✉ Above Groppi, 28 Shari' Mahmoud Basyouni, Downtown ☎ 02-2575 0822
🕐 7am–2am

Kebabgi (££)
Excellent grilled meat dishes served with a large selection of *mezze*, on a splendid Nile terrace.

✉ Sofitel Gezirah, 3 Shari' al Thawra Council, Gezira ☎ 02-2737 3737
🕐 Daily 11:30am–midnight

La Mezzaluna (££)

Popular with locals and full of atmosphere, Mezzaluna serves good Italian cuisine and fabulous salads, but it's also a great place for a coffee.

✉ Shari' Aziz Osman, Zamalik ☎ 02-2735 2655 🕐 Daily 7am–11pm

Moghul Room (£££)

A good place to recover from a hectic day, this elegant and beautifully decorated restaurant serves authentic Indian food, with soothing live Indian music every night.

✉ Mena House Oberoi Hotel, Shari' al Ahram, near the Giza Pyramids
☎ 02-3377 3222 🕐 Daily 7:30–midnight, also Fri lunchtime

Naguib Mahfouz Coffee Shop (£)

See page 59.

Revolving Restaurant (£££)

Located on the 41st floor, this is undoubtedly the restaurant with the best view in Cairo, and the food is superb, too. It is set around the show kitchen where you can see the chefs whip up culinary delights from all over the world. Formal dress. Book in advance.

✉ Grand Hyatt Hotel, on the Corniche, Garden City ☎ 02-2365 1234
🕐 7pm–1am

Sabaya (££–£££)

The best Lebanese restaurant in town with a great variety of *mezze*, including several different *kibbeh nayyeh* (raw pounded lamb). Peaceful, modern Oriental decor and extremely good service from the truly delightful waiters.

✉ Semiramis InterContinental, Corniche al Nil, Garden City ☎ 02-2795 7171
🕐 7:30pm–1am

Samakmak (££)

There is no menu, you can just select your fish from the catch of the day, have it fried or grilled, and it will be served with rice, bread and salads. After a delicious meal, you can relax with a waterpipe while overlooking Cairo traffic. Take-out or delivery is available.

✉ 24 Shari' Ahmed Orabi, Mohandiseen ☎ 02-3302 7308 🕓 Noon–4am

Seasons (£££)

One of the best restaurants in the area, set in an elegant interior that reminds more of Manhattan than Cairo, but then the Nile is just there outside. The eclectic menu offers superb food that is beautifully presented. Excellent service too.

✉ Four Seasons Hotel, 35 Giza Street ☎ 02-2573 1212 🕓 11:30am–1am

Sequoia (££)

The hip place in town, this lounge/bar/restaurant is the place to be seen sipping cocktails, eating good reasonably priced *mezze* and smoking a waterpipe.

✉ 3 Shari' Abu al Fida, Zamalik ☎ 02-2576 8086 🕓 1pm–1am

Simmonds Coffee Shop (£)

Good place for a breakfast pastry at the bar, washed down with fresh fruit juice, and for coffee all day.

✉ 112 Shari' 26 July, Zamalik ☎ 02-2735 9436 🕓 7am–10pm

Villa Belle Epoque Restaurant (£££)

A delicious gourmet French-international cuisine with local flavours is served in the cool and elegant conservatory-turned-dining-space and lush garden.

✉ Road 13, Villa 63, Maadi ☎ 02-2358 0265; www.villabelleepoque.com
🕓 1pm–10.30pm

SHOPPING

BOOKSHOPS

AUC Bookshop

The most extensive range of books on Egypt and the Middle East, many published by the American University Press, as well as the latest English literature.

✉ Shari' Sheikh Rihan, corner of Midan Tahrir, Downtown ☎ 02-2797 5929;
www.aucpress.com
✉ 16 Shari' Mohammed Thakeb, Zamalik ☎ 02-2739 7045

Diwan

Excellent store with books in English and Arabic, a good kids section, DVDs and CDs. Visitors can browse in the small cafe that serves home-made cakes and drinks. Very good selection.

✉ 159 Shari' 26 July, Zamalik ☎ 02-2736 2578;
www.diwanegypt.com

Lehnert and Landrock

Wonderful German, English and French bookshop with a large section on ancient and modern Egypt, Islam and the Arab world. You can also purchase copies of interesting old photographs of Cairo and Upper Egypt, new and old postcards and other Egyptian paraphernalia.

✉ 44 Shari' Sherif, Downtown ☎ 02-2393 7606

L'Orientaliste

Great but expensive bookshop packed full of dusty first editions and more valuable second-hand books and old maps about Egypt, Orientalism or the Middle East in general.

✉ 15 Shari' Qasr al Nil ☎ 02-2575 3418; www.orientalecairo.com

Zamalik Bookstore

A good bookshop with mainly books on Egypt in European languages, foreign newspapers and magazines and stationery.

✉ 19 Shari' Shagaret al Dor, Zamalik ☎ 02-2736 9197

CLOTHES AND FABRICS
Atlas Silks

This tiny shop continues a long tradition of making exquisite moiré fabrics in a wide variety of colours as well as tailoring clothes in both Oriental and Western styles. It also makes shoes in the same fabric.

✉ Sikket al Badestan, Khan al Khalili ☎ 02-2591 8833

Al Khiyamiya (Tentmakers Bazaar)

Well-preserved roofed market, where the traditional crafts of appliqué work and tentmaking are still practised. You can order one of the magnificent tents in a patchwork of Islamic designs, or just a cushion cover or wallhanging for a child's room.

✉ Just outside Bab Zuwayla, Islamic Cairo

Mohamed Abdo

Mohamed Abdo's showroom is filled with glittering, intricately designed dresses as well as belts, head ornaments, brass cymbals and jewellery. Belly dancers try out the outfits in front of a mirror while performing moves to the loud accompaniment of the latest belly-dance CDs.

✉ 50C Khan al Khalili, Islamic Cairo ☎ 019-524-0395; www.swayonthemoon.jeeran.com

Nagada

Beautiful hand-woven cotton fabrics, clothes and tablecloths in natural colours, fabric lanterns and fabulous pottery made in the village of Tunes in Al Faiyum are all tastefully displayed here.

✉ 13 Shari' Refa'a, Dokki ☎ 02-3748 6663; www.nagada.net

Ouf

A wide range of cheap cotton clothing, funky flowery fabrics, bed sheets, tablecloths and Bedouin-style embroidered dresses is on sale here.

✉ First alley to the left off the Spice Bazaar, which is the alley running along the Madrasa of Sultan Barsbey, off Shari' al Mu'Izz li-Din Allah

Tanis

Wonderful cotton and linen fabrics, mostly for furnishings, carrying modern interpretations of pharaonic motifs or simply camels and palm trees. Look out for the attractive curtain gauze, with Arabic calligraphy or Ottoman star and crescents printed white on white.

✉ 9 Shari' Mohamed Anis, Zamalik ☎ 02-2737 2555

HANDICRAFTS
Al Ain Gallery

This gallery exhibits Azza Fahmy's wonderful contemporary silver jewellery, decorated with Arabic inscriptions, as well as traditional metal work, including lanterns and lighting by Randa Fahmy.

✉ 73 Shari' al Hussayn, Dokki, Cairo ☎ 02-2791 7000; www.azzafahmy.com

Dr Ragab's Papyrus Institute

This institute was founded by former ambassador Dr Hassan Ragab, who revived the making of papyrus to help preserve and promote this ancient Egyptian art. The museum displays the different stages of the making of papyrus and has a sales room on the first floor where you can buy top-quality papyri at top prices.

✉ Shari' al Nil, close to the Cairo Sheraton, Giza ☎ 02-2336 72127

Egypt Crafts Center/Fairtrade Egypt

This non-profit-making organization sells and promotes Egyptian crafts, from kilims and embroidered clothes from Northern Sinai to hand-woven tablecloths from Akhmim, recycled paper from Cairo and colourful baskets from Aswan. These high-quality products bear no relation to what is on sale in tatty tourist bazaars.

✉ 1st floor, apt 8, 27 Shari' Yahia Ibrahim, Zamalik, Cairo ☎ 02-2736 5123; www.fairtradeegypt.org

Hareem Khan

Small jewellery store in the heart of Khan al Khalili selling old and reproduced Bedouin jewellery in silver with brightly coloured semi-precious stones and enamel work.

✉ 6 Shari' al Haramitiya, Khan al Khalili, Cairo ☎ 02-2593 1581

Khan Misr Tulun

A wonderful treasure trove filled with some of the best handicrafts from all over Egypt, including the villages and oases. The stock sold is world away from most of what is on sale in Khan al Khalili including embroidered textiles, hand-blown glass and ceramics.

✉ Facing the main entrance of the Ibn Tulun Mosque, Sayyida Zaynab, Cairo ☎ 02-2365 2227 🕐 Mon–Sat 10–5. Closed Sun

Nomad Gallery

A floor of an elegant Zamalik residence is filled with original Bedouin jewellery and rugs, as well as traditional designs in silver, and textiles and many types of baskets, mostly hand-made in Egypt.

✉ 1st floor, 14 Saraya al Gezira, Zamalik (and smaller branch in garden of the Cairo Marriott Hotel, Zamalik) ☎ 02-2736 1917

Oum al Dounia
Great Downtown store for one-stop shopping, with a book store and Egyptian crafts from all over the country.

✉ 1st floor, 3 Shari' Tal'At Harb, Downtown ☎ 02-2393 8273
🕐 Daily 10–7

Pottery School of Michel and Evelyne Pastore
This Swiss couple of potters started a pottery school for local children in this artists' village. You can see them at work or buy their fabulous pottery from the shop.

✉ Village of Tunis, on the road to Wadi al Ruwayan, along Qarun Lake, Al Faiyum ☎ 02-3748 6663; www.nagada.net

Al Qahira
This new stylish store sells the works of local artisans, including funky furniture, lamps, clothing, bags with Umm Kalthoum and movie stars and beautiful wooden inlaid boxes.

✉ 1st floor, 6 Shari' Bahgat Ali, Zamalik ☎ No phone 🕐 Mon–Sat 11–9

Ramses Wissa Wassef
This arts centre has been weaving carpets since 1952 and its work has been admired and collected by museums and galleries around the world. The carpets are woven by villagers under the eye of different generations of the Wissa Wassef family.

✉ Off the Saqqara Road, 4km (2.5 miles) south of Giza, Harraniya, Cairo
☎ 02-3381 5746; www.wissawassef.com 🕐 Daily 10–5

Townhouse Gallery
The best contemporary art gallery in the city, in a town house right next to the factory. You can pick up books, crafts and art.

✉ Shari' Hussein al Me'mar, off Shari' Mahmoud Bassyouni, Downtown
☎ 02-2576 8086; www.thetownhousegallery.com

ENTERTAINMENT

NIGHTLIFE

Absolute

Great disco and lounge bar with excellent DJs, and views of the Nile. It's expensive but worth going to but it does get busy on a Thursday or Friday night.

✉ Casino Al Shagara, Corniche al Nil, Bulaq, opposite the World Trade Centre, Cairo ☎ 02-2579 6512 🕓 9pm–3am

Cairo Jazz Club

Although in an unlikely place, the Cairo Jazz Club hosts regular live jazz sessions from foreign and Egyptian musicians. There's always a great atmosphere. Serves good *mezze* and salads, too.

✉ 197, 26 July Street, beside the Zamalik Bridge, Aguza, Cairo
☎ 02-3345 9939; www.cairojazzclub.com 🕓 5pm–3am

Mojo Lounge

On the top-deck of an ex-Nile cruiser, this lounge is a great place for a drink or some Mediterranean cuisine and a waterpipe.

✉ Imperial Boat, 4 Shari' Sarayat Al Gezira, Zamalik ☎ 010-222 3999; www.mojothelounge.com 🕓 Sun–Wed 11am–1am; Thu–Sat 11am–2am

Al Morocco

This bar-restaurant turns into a disco later at night, very popular with young wealthy Cairenes, who dance to Western and Egyptian music. Outside seating area if you want to escape the crowds.

✉ Blue Nile boat, 9 Saray al Gezira, Zamalik, Cairo ☎ 02-2735 3114

Palmyra

Many a belly dancer starts out at the Palmyra, a 1950s, dark and somewhat sleazy nightclub, where the dancing gets better the later it gets.

✉ Alley off 26 July Street, Ezbekiya 🕓 10pm–4am

THEATRE AND LIVE MUSIC

After Eight

See page 106.

At Tannoura Dance Troup

At Tannoura, Egypt's only Sufi dance troupe, perform in this great medieval space.

⊠ Wikalat al Ghuri ☎ 02-2512 1735 🕒 May–Sep Mon, Wed, Sat 8pm; Oct–Apr 7pm 🎟 Free

Beit al Harrawi

Various performances of Arabic music and theatre particularly during the Ramadan nights. On the first Thursday of every month there is a free classical Arabic music concert.

⊠ Behind Al Azhar Mosque, Islamic Cairo ☎ 02-2510 4174

Cairo Opera House

The main hall features Egyptian and prestigious international ballet, opera and theatre performances. The smaller hall features Egyptian performances. Advance booking is recommended. Men should wear jacket and tie for all performances.

⊠ Gezira Exhibition Grounds, Gezira, Cairo ☎ 02-2739 8144; www.operahouse.gov.eg

Al Genaina Theatre

Excellent open-air theatre for Western-style performances and regular concerts.

⊠ Al Azhar Park, Shari' Salah Salem ☎ 02-2362 6748; www.mawred.org

Makan

Great space that does research and promotes traditional Egyptian music. There are musical evenings on Tuesdays and Wednesdays.

⊠ 1 Shari' Saad Zaghloul, Al Mounira, Downtown ☎ 02-2792 0878; www.egyptmusic.org 🕒 Tue, Wed 9pm

Al-Sawy Cultural Center

Very active centre with performances every night of experimental theatre, Arabic music or jazz concerts, lectures and screenings of films and documentaries.

⊠ Shari' 26 July, Zamalik, under the bridge to Agouza, Cairo ☎ 02-2736 6178; www.culturewheel.com

Alexandria, the Northwest and the Oases

Alexandria has always been Egypt's link to the Mediterranean world, but since many of its foreign residents left in the 1950s and '60s, the city has become increasingly conservative and Egyptian. Both Mersa Matruh, a trading post where Greeks traded with the northern Bedouin, and Rosetta (Rashid), popular with foreigners in the mid-19th century, are now also resolutely Egyptian towns.

Al Iskandarîa (Alexandria) □

Siwa Oasis

Baharîya Oasis

Farâfra Oasis

Dâkhla Oasis

Khârga Oasis

The western oases and particularly Siwa have a very distinct character, cut off as they are from the Nile Valley and the coast. Surrounded by the huge expanses of desert, and until last century visited regularly only by camel caravans, their main income still comes from the palm groves and olive trees. Change is coming fast, though, with the Egyptian government's interest in resettling people from the Nile Valley, as well as the growth of desert tourism.

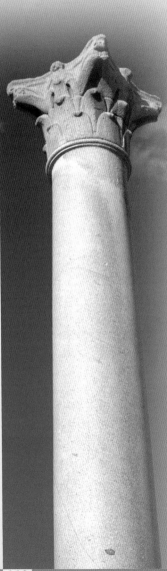

ALEXANDRIA

Alexandria (Al Iskandaria), Egypt's second-largest city, was famous throughout the classical world as a place of learning and of academic achievement – its icon was the Pharos, a lighthouse, one of the seven wonders of the world.

Centuries after its heyday, when conquered by the Arabs in AD641 it was still described as a marble city of 4,000 palaces and 400 theatres.

Little of ancient Alexandria is visible in the city, but exciting finds have been made in the Eastern harbour, including remains of Cleopatra's Palace and the Pharos. The Bibliotheca Alexandrina was built in memory of the famous ancient library, the Mouseion, which was entirely destroyed. It has put the focus back on Alexandria as a cultural city.
✚ 4A

Amud al Sawari (Pompey's Pillar) and Serapeum

Pompey's Pillar is one of Alexandria's most famous landmarks. The Crusaders wrongly attributed this 27m-high (88ft) pink granite column to Pompey. It was erected for Diocletian around AD295, probably to support his equestrian statue. The hill on which it stands was ancient Rhakotis, where Alexander the Great first established Alexandria.

The Serapeum and the great Alexandrian Library developed into a major centre of learning under the Ptolemies, and remained so until the fourth century, when the Christians burned everything down. The pillar and two granite sphinxes are all that remain.

✉ Shari' Amud al Sawari ☎ 03-960 1315 ✪ Daily 9–4:30 ✋ Inexpensive

Bibliotheca Alexandrina

Inspired by the ancient library founded in the third century BC, the new library is designed to hold eight million books. The collection is far from complete, but the complex already receives about 1.5 million visitors each year. The circular design evokes the sun rising again on this side of the Mediterranean. The complex includes an Impressions of Alexandria exhibit illustrating the city's history with maps, drawings and photographs, a Manuscript Museum, a small Antiquities Museum with objects from the Graeco-Roman Museum, a Planetarium and an excellent concert hall.

www.bibalex.org

✉ Corniche al Bahr ☎ 03-483 9999 ✪ Sun–Thu 11–7, Fri, Sat 3–7
🚍 Microbus along Corniche ✋ Expensive; combined ticket for all museums

Kom al Dikka (Roman Odeon)

Alexandria's multi-layered history can be seen at Kom al Dikka (Arabic for pile of rubble). Beneath late-Roman ruins, ninth- and tenth-century Muslim tombs and a late 18th-century fort, archaeologists revealed an elegant second-century AD amphitheatre with seating for 750 people. Alexandrians enjoyed musical performances and wrestling contests at this pretty Roman theatre. The mosaic flooring in the forecourt originally covered the whole area. The Villa of the Birds (separate entrance ticket; inexpensive), near the theatre, has a beautifully restored mosaic floor with nine panels depicting colourful birds.

✉ Behind Cinema Amir, off Shari' Salman Yusuf ☎ 03-486 5106 🕓 Daily 9–5 ✋ Inexpensive; separate ticket for Villa: inexpensive

Kom al Shogafa Catacombs

The catacombs at Kom al Shogafa (Hill of Tiles) are unique both in plan and decoration, an unusual blend of ancient Egyptian, Greek

and Roman designs which epitomized classical Alexandria's cosmopolitanism. The original second-century-AD family vault was later enlarged to take in the community, creating the largest Roman funerary complex found in Egypt.

The catacombs are on three levels, but the lowest floor is now inaccessible to visitors because of flooding. A wide staircase, lit by a central well through which corpses were lowered, leads through the first-floor vestibule to the Rotunda, where eight pillars support a domed roof, the Banquet Hall (to the left) and the Hall of Caracalla (to the right) with four painted tombs. A small spiral staircase leads to the eerie second-level tombs, which have wonderful decorations of bearded serpents, Medusas, a falcon Horus and the Egyptian gods Anubis and Sobek dressed as Roman soldiers.

✉ Off Shari' Amud al Sawari, Karmuz ☎ 03-484 5800 ⏰ Daily 9–5 ✋ Moderate

Mathaf Cavafy (Cavafy Museum)

The apartment where the famous Greek poet Constantine Cavafy (1863–1933) lived for the last 25 years of his life has become a museum. "Where could I live better?" he said. "Below, the brothel caters for the flesh. And there is the church which forgives sin. And there is the hospital where we die."

His furniture, icons, death mask, books and the desk at which he wrote some of his greatest poetry, including *The City* and *The Barbarians*, can be seen.

✉ 4 Shari' Sharm el Sheikh, off Shari' Sultan Hussein ☎ 03-486 1598 ⏰ Tue–Sun 10–4. Closed Mon ✋ Inexpensive

a walk in downtown Alexandria

Start at the Bibliotheca Alexandrina (➤ 119) and walk west along the Corniche. Go past the Cecil Hotel to the Tomb of the Unknown Soldier, then turn left.

This is the heart of the old European Alexandria, marked by an equestrian statue of Muhammad Ali.

At Midan al Tahrir turn left along Shari' Salah Salem.

Note the Moorish Anglican Church of St Mark and the National Bank of Egypt, a copy of Palazzo Farnese in Rome.

Continue along Shari' Fouad and at Patisserie Venous turn right into Shari' Nabi Danyal.

Half-way up the street, on the left, is Nabi Danyal Mosque, built over a cistern, which some believe contains Alexander the Great's tomb.

Turn left into Shari' Yussef with the Roman Odeon (▶ 120) on your left. After a visit continue along the same street and turn left round the site of the theatre. Cross the road into Shari' Zangalola.

This leads to the Greek Orthodox Church of St Saba.

Follow the street to the left of the church and then turn into the first street to the right, Shari' Sharm el Sheikh. The Cavafy Museum is at No 4 (▶ 121). Walk left out of the museum, turn left onto Shari' Sultan Hussein, and then right into Shari' Nabi Danyal.

You will pass the Coptic Cathedral of St Mark (on the left) and Alexandria's neo-classical synagogue (on the right).

Continue along the street back to Midan Zaghloul.

Distance 2.5km (1.5 miles)
Time 2.5 hours without visits, 4 hours with visits
Start point Bibliotheca Alexandrina, Corniche al Bahr
End point Midan Saad Zaghloul
Lunch Cap d'Or (£–££) ✉ 4 Shari' Adib, off Shari' Saad Zaghloul; tel: 03-487 5177

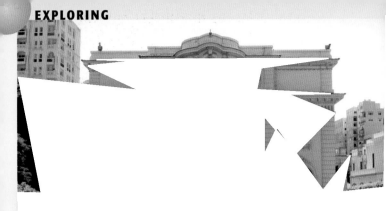

Al Mathaf al Dawli (National Museum of Alexandria)

The National Museum of Alexandria, set in a beautiful white Italianate villa in Alexandria's city centre, is the first of a line of museums in important Egyptian cities. Its aim is to reveal the city's long and specific history, from antiquity until the modern period, through the very well displayed and labelled artefacts that have come from several of the city's other museums.

The collection is laid out over three floors, the first of which is devoted to the Pharaonic period. The second floor displays artefacts from the Graeco-Roman period and the top floor is devoted to Coptic, Muslim and modern Alexandria. Highlights include the sphinx and other sculpture found in the Eastern harbour, Roman death masks, the small but elegant Tanagra terracotta statues and a bronze sculpture of Harpocrates in a mixed Greek and Egyptian style. Every room has several interesting panels explaining about ancient Egyptian rituals and gods, as well as the development of religion, art and history through the ages.

www.alexmuseum.org.eg

✉ 110 Tariq al Hurreya ☎ 03-483 5519 🕓 Daily 9–4:30 ✋ Moderate

Mathaf Mahmoud Said

Mahmoud Said (1897–1964) was one of Egypt's finest 20th-century artists. About 40 of his unusual works, including his stunning Egyptian nudes, are beautifully exhibited in his own Italianate villa. Displayed on the first floor are the works of two of his contemporaries Saif and Adham Wanli, while a Museum of Modern Art fills the basement.

✉ 6 Shari' Mohammed Said Pasha, Gianaclis ☎ 03-582 1688 🕐 Sat–Thu 9–1:30, 5–9 ✋ Inexpensive 🚌 Tram 2 to San Stefano stop

Qasr al Muntazah (Muntazah Palace)

Khedive Abbas II's extravagant Turko-Florentine palace may be closed to the public, but the vast, beautiful gardens are a popular day trip for Alexandrian families and are well worth a visit. The private Muntazah beach is one of the most pleasant near Alexandria, separated from Ma'amoura bay by a pretty Turkish-style belvedere.

✉ Muntazah Bay ✋ Inexpensive
🍴 Fast food restaurants (£), restaurants at Helnan Palestine and Salamlek hotels (£££) 🚐 Microbus on Corniche to Muntazah

Qal'at Qaytbay (Qaytbay Fort)

The fabled lighthouse or Pharos of Alexandria, one of the Seven Wonders of the ancient world, was built in 279BC by Sostratus for Ptolemy II. It was reputedly over 125m (410ft) high and had over 300 rooms. The lighthouse was completely destroyed by earthquakes in the 11th and 14th centuries, but excavations have revealed several fragements of it. In 1479, Sultan Qaytbay built his fort on the site, reusing some of the Pharos' stones and columns, notably in the west-facing outer wall. The fort has great views from the walls. Part of the fort is now open as a Marine Museum, with displays and aquariums housing fish from the Mediterranean and the Red Sea.

✉ End of the Corniche ☎ 03-486 5106 🕒 Daily 9–4; closed Fri 11:30–1:30 🚌 Microbus along Corniche ♿ Inexpensive

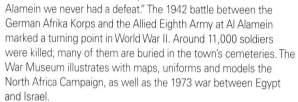

The Northwest

AL ALAMEIN

Winston Churchill wrote: "Before Alamein we never had a victory. After Alamein we never had a defeat." The 1942 battle between the German Afrika Korps and the Allied Eighth Army at Al Alamein marked a turning point in World War II. Around 11,000 soldiers were killed; many of them are buried in the town's cemeteries. The War Museum illustrates with maps, uniforms and models the North Africa Campaign, as well as the 1973 war between Egypt and Israel.

➕ 3B ✉ 106km (66 miles) west of Alexandria ☎ 046-410 0031 (museum) 🕐 Museum daily 9–4; Commonwealth War Cemetery daily 7–2:30 ✋ Museum inexpensive; cemeteries free 🍴 Restaurant (£) at Max 24, east of War Museum 🚌 Buses from Alexandria to Mersa Matruh stop 200m from the War Museum, but no transport to the cemeteries

MERSA MATRUH

Mersa Matruh has grown from a sleepy fishing town into a sprawling, dull summer resort for Egyptian holidaymakers. The superb beaches get overcrowded in summer, but are quiet for the rest of the year. The closest beach is Rommel Beach, where the legendary German Field Marshall Erwin Rommel, nicknamed "The Desert Fox" for leading the Afrika Korps to amazing victories over the British, reputedly went for a swim. The better beaches are west of town: Cleopatra's Beach (7km/4 miles), Al Obeid Beach (20km/12 miles) and the splendid Agibah Beach (28km/17 miles) with deep turquoise water. The Rommel Museum, in a cave behind the port, has a collection of Rommel's memorabilia.

➕ 1A (off map) ✉ 290km (180 miles) from Alexandria, 512km (318 miles) from Cairo 🍴 Abdu Kofta, Shari' al Tahrir; tel: 012-314 4989 🚌 Buses from Cairo and Alexandria ✈ Domestic flights from Cairo ℹ Corner of Shari' Omar Mukhtar/the Corniche; tel: 046-493 1841

ROSETTA (RASHID)

During the Ottoman era, Rosetta had a larger port than Alexandria. Today the town is rather neglected, but the 22 surviving grand mansions bear witness to its glory days. Most of the houses, built in Delta-style architecture with red and black brickwork and elaborate wooden screens, have been restored or are under restoration. One of the finest, Ramadan House on Shari' Port Said, can be visited inside, while the neighbouring 18th-century houses can be admired from the outside. From there, walk downhill and take the second street to the left for more stunning architecture from the House of al Toqati, House of Abu Shaheen and the superb House of Amasyali with wonderful painted ceilings.

Five kilometres (3 miles) outside, Qaytbay's 15th-century fort marks the end of the Nile's 5,440km-long (3,380-mile) run from East Africa into the Mediterranean. Near here, in 1799, a French officer discovered a second-century BC basalt stone with inscriptions in three scripts – hieroglyphs, demotic and Greek. It was from this Rosetta Stone (now in London's British Museum) that French scholar Jean François Champollion deciphered ancient Egyptian hieroglyphs.

🚌 5A 🖂 64km (40 miles) east of Alexandria 🕐 Houses and fort daily 9–4, Fri closed 12–1:30 💷 Inexpensive (tickets can be bought at the tourist office) 🍴 Cafes (£) on main street
🚌 Hourly bus from Alexandria, Midan al Gumhuriya
ℹ️ Main square at Tourist Police office; tel: 045-292 1733

WADI AL NATRUN

Although monasticism started in the Eastern Desert, it was in Wadi al Natrun that the rules were

developed. For the last 1,500 years the Coptic popes have been chosen from these monasteries. The current pope, Shenuda III, formerly a monk at Deir al Suryani, has encouraged a monastic revival. St Bishoi (AD320–407) was one of the earliest monks in Wadi al Natrun and his monastery still has more than 100 monks and hermits. His body is said to be perfectly preserved in his tomb here. Deir al Suryani was founded in the sixth-century by displeased monks from Deir Anba Bishoi and later taken over by Syrian monks. Deir al Suryani's Church of the Virgin was built around a fourth-century cave where St Bishoi prayed, and has some magnificent 11th-century wall-paintings. The oldest and most remote of the monasteries is Deir al Baramus, founded by two sons of Emperor Valentine who died during their fasting. Deir al Maqar was founded by St Makarius, who died in AD390 after spending 60 years as a hermit in the desert. This is where most Coptic popes are buried and, unless you have permission to visit, it is closed to the public.

✚ 5C ✉ 105km (65 miles) from Cairo, off Alexandria Desert Road 🕓 Call for opening times: Deir Anba Bishoi (tel: 02-2591 4448), Deir al Suryani and Deir al Baramus (tel: 02-2592 9658), Deir al Maqar (tel: 02-2577 0614) 💵 Donations appreciated 🍴 Wadi Natrun Resthouse (£–££) on Desert Road 🚌 Buses between Cairo and Alexandria to the Resthouse, and from there regular pick-ups to the monasteries ❓ Some monasteries close during the five seasons of Lent (dates variable)

The Oases

The Western Desert, covering some 3 million sq km (1,158,000sq miles), runs from the Mediterranean south to Kordofan in Central Sudan, and from the Nile Valley west to Fezzan in Libya.

BAHARIYA

On the main street of Bahariya's main town, Al Bawiti, is the Oasis Heritage Museum, with exhibits on Bedouin life and a little shop selling excellent local crafts. A new museum houses some of the Golden Mummies found in the oasis in 1996, dating back to the Graeco-Roman period. In the middle of the gardens (used to cultivate fruit trees) are the Roman Al Bishnu springs; however, these are not recommended for bathing. Instead, take a day trip to some of the desert springs or spend a night in the amazing White Desert or Black Desert en route to Farafra. Amid the houses in Al Bawiti is Qarat Qasr Salim, with two very rich 26th-Dynasty tombs containing fascinating wall decorations, now open to the public.

✚ 2F ✉ 360km (223 miles) from Cairo 🍴 Cafes/restaurant (£) 🚌 Daily buses to Cairo from Turgoman bus station. Buses to Farafra and Dakhla

DAKHLA

Mut, the ancient and modern capital, has a small Ethnographic Museum, with scenes of life in the oases, and hot springs believed to cure colds and rheumatism. Al Qasr, about 30km (18 miles) from Mut, is Dakhla's medieval capital of three-storey mudbrick houses. The Ayyubid Nasr al Din Mosque is notable for its 21m-high (70ft) wooden minaret. Five kilometres (3 miles) further west are the beautifully decorated 1st- and 2nd-century-AD Muwazaka Tombs and 2km (1.2 miles) from there, the 1st-century-AD Roman temple of Deir al Haggar.

✚ 13M (off map) ✉ 310km (192 miles) from Farafra 🎫 Museum: Sat–Thu 8–2 ✋ Sights inexpensive 🍴 Cafes (£) 🚌 Daily buses from Cairo, Asyut, Kharga, Farafra, Bahariya

ℹ Shari' Et-Thaura al Khadra, Mut; tel: 092-782 1685

FARAFRA

Qasr Farafra is the only settlement in this most beautiful and remote oasis, with a small, pretty mudbrick museum built by local artist Badr. Walking in the peaceful palm groves and lovely gardens makes up for a lack of ancient monuments.

✚ 2F (off map) ✉ 180km (112 miles) from Al Bawiti, Bahariya 🍴 A few restaurants (£) 🚌 Daily buses from Cairo, Bahariya and Dakhla ❓ Tours to the White Desert from Al Waha Hotel

KHARGA

Modern Kharga town has borne the brunt of the government's New Valley development and has little charm, although the Kharga Museum of Antiquities is worth visiting to see the displays of local artefacts. North of the town, beyond the ruined Ptolemaic temple of Nadura, stands one of Egypt's few surviving Persian monuments, the sixth-century BC Temple of Hibis, dedicated to Amun-Re. Near by is the impressive Bagawat necropolis, with finely decorated Christian chapels from the third to seventh centuries AD. North of the necropolis, and only accessible by car, are two superb Roman fortresses and some aqueducts.

✚ 13M (off map) ✉ 195km (121 miles) from Dakhla 🎫 Museum daily 8–5; temples and necropolis daily 8–6 (8–5 in winter) 🍴 Hotel restaurants (£–££) 🚌 Daily buses from Cairo, Asyut and other oases 🚆 Fri train to Luxor

ℹ Midan Nasser; tel: 092-792 1206

SIWA

Siwa Town is still a sleepy, relaxed sort of place, despite the increase in visitors in recent years. The Traditional Siwan House shows what most Siwan houses looked like before breeze block arrived. The new town lies in the shadow of abandoned Shali, the mudbrick hilltop town founded in 1203 and fortified against Bedouin attacks, which is floodlit at night. Alexander the Great came to Siwa in 331BC to consult the Oracle at the ancient settlement of Aghurmi, 3km (2 miles) east of the modern town. The 26th Dynasty Temple of the Oracle dedicated to Amun-Re has survived well. From the minaret of Aghurmi's Mosque there are excellent views of this picturesque settlement, inhabited until the early 20th century, and over towards the nearby temple of Umm Ubayda. The salt lake Birket Siwa and Futnas Island are a favourite picnic spot and a good place to swim. The main attractions of Siwa however are the vast palm groves and the spectacular nearby Great Sand Sea, with its high perfect sand dunes and cold and hot water springs.

🕂 1A (off map)

✉ 300km (186 miles) south of Mersa Matruh

🍴 Cafes/restaurants (£–££) 🚌 2 daily buses from Mersa Matruh and Alexandria ❓ Siwa Festival 3 days in October just before the date harvest; Traditional Siwan House is open Sun–Thu 9am–2:30pm

ℹ Siwa town, on the Matruh Road; tel: 046-460 1338/010-546 1992

HOTELS

ALEXANDRIA

Cecil (££)

This famous and once grand hotel has been stripped of much of its character over the years, and now is only a shadow of its former self. The rooms are fine though, the views over the Med are great and it is very central.

✉ Midan Saad Zaghloul ☎ 03-487 7173; www.sofitel.com

Egypt Hotel (£–££)

Set in a renovated Italianate building in the centre of Alexandria, this hotel offers comfortable rooms with en-suite bathrooms, and a little balcony with sea view.

✉ 1 Shari' Degla ☎ 03-481 4483

Et Tarfa Desert Lodge & Spa (£££)

Traditional mud-brick architecture with 20 wonderful individual rooms, set against a backdrop of gorgeous desert dunes. This is the perfect place to relax and offers a whole new concept of luxury in the desert.

✉ Al Mansoura, Al Qasr, Dakhla ☎ 092-910 5007; http://altarfalodge.com

Four Seasons Alexandria (£££)

The most luxurious hotel in town, Four Seasons overlooks San Stefano Beach. The hotel has 118 spacious and elegant rooms, each with a private balcony overlooking the Mediterranean, a European-style spa, several excellent restaurants and a trendy shopping mall.

✉ 399 Corniche, San Stefano ☎ 03-581 8000; www.fourseasons.com/alexandria

Metropole (££)

Period hotel with charming high-ceilinged rooms and lots of atmosphere. Excellent and friendly service. Serious competition for the neighbouring Cecil. Reserve ahead.

✉ 52 Shari' Saad Zaghloul ☎ 03-486 1467; www.paradiseinnegypt.com

Windsor Palace (££)
Built in 1907, the Windsor is another of the city's restored old-style hotels. The hotel has a grand lobby and comfortable and large rooms, the more expensive ones overlooking the Mediterranean.
✉ Shari' esh-Shouhada, Corniche al Bahr ☎ 03-480 8123; www.paradiseinnegypt.com

THE OASES
Adrere Amellal (£££)
Delightful desert eco-lodge set in its own oasis at the edge of the salt lake. Every room is different, built in the traditional mud and salt, lit by candlelight (no electricity) and the pool flows out of a Roman spring. The delcious food from the organic garden is served on old family china.
✉ Sidi Jaafar, outside Siwa Town ☎ 02-2736 7879; www.adrereamellal.net

Al Badawiya Safari and Hotel (£)
Tastefully designed in mudbrick, the clean, domed rooms have private or shared bathrooms. Owned by local Bedouins, but run by a Swiss woman. Book in advance.
✉ Main street, Farafra ☎ 092-751 0060/012-214 8343; www.badawiya.com

Desert Lodge (££–£££)
Traditionally designed eco-lodge overlooking the old town of al Qasr and the desert, with lovely rooms with air conditioning and private bathrooms.
✉ Al Qasr, Dakhla ☎ 092-772 7061; www.desertlodge.net

Old Oasis Hotel (£–££)
A pleasant hotel on the edge of a palm grove opposite a hot spring, that feeds the swimming pool. The simple but lovely rooms surround a palm-shaded garden. It is just a 10-minute walk from main street al Bawiti in Bahariya.
✉ Al Beshmo spring, Bahariyya ☎ 012-232 4425; www.oldoasissafari.com

Pioneers Hotel (£££)

The Pioneers has the most comfortable air-conditioned rooms and there is a large swimming pool and a children's play area. Same owners as the equally salmon-pink painted, three-star Mut Talata in Dakhla (tel: 092-821 530).

✉ Kharga ☎ 092-792 7982; www.solymar.com

Shali Lodge (££)

This small mud-brick hotel, set in its palm grove, is under the same management as the Adrere Amellal, with peaceful rooms around a small pool.

✉ Shari' Subukha, Siwa ☎ 046-460 1299

Taziry Ecolodge (£–££)

Lovely hotel run by a couple of Alexandrian artists, with cosy rooms decorated with local crafts and Bedouin rugs, and a natural spring pool, all overlooking the lake.

✉ Sidi Jaafar, White Mountain, Siwa ☎ 02-12 340 8492; www.taziry.com

RESTAURANTS

ALEXANDRIA
Cap d'Or (£–££)

This atmospheric bar-restaurant is one of the few remaining reminders of Alexandria's old Greek tavernas. Try the calamari stew with a cool beer, while listening to 1970s French *chanson* or people watching.

✉ 4 Shari' Adib, off Shari' Saad Zagloul ☎ 03-487 5177
🕐 10am–3am

Centro de Portugal (££)

Excellent food to please the many expats who hang out here, from peppery steak with good chips, the house special, to pasta and grilled fish, all served in a lovely garden. There is a great selection of cocktails and icy beers.

✉ 42 Shari' Abd al Kader, off Shari' Kafr Abdou ☎ 03-542 7599
🕐 3pm–1am 🗓 Admission to club 10LE

Coffee Roastery (£–££)

Trendy American-style cafe-restaurant where young Alexandrians and families with small children like to meet up over a coffee or a milkshake. Also serves good snacks and Western-style dishes. MTV is on all day and the place seems wired day and night.

✉ 48 Shari' Fuad ☎ 03-483 4363 🕔 7am–2am

Fish Market (££–£££)

See page 59.

Greek Club (Club Nautique Héllenique) (£–££)

The best place to watch the sunset is on the long breezy terrace overlooking the Eastern Harbour, with an icy cold beer and a simple but very fresh grilled fish with a salad.

✉ Shari' Qasr Qait Bay, Anfushi ☎ 03-480 2690 🕔 Noon–11pm

Samakmak (££)

Near the fish market, this unpretentious restaurant is what you'd expect a fish restaurant to be. There is indoor and outdoor seating, and the very fresh fish you choose from the counter is grilled or fried as you wish.

✉ 42 Qasr Ras et Tin, Bahari ☎ 03-481 1560 🕔 Noon–2am

Spitfire Bar (£)

Popular 1970s bar, playing good old rock 'n' roll and filled to the brim with memorabilia and pictures from loyal customers, including American sailors, many of whom like to drop in when at anchor.

✉ 7 Shari' al Bursa al Qadima ☎ 03-480 6503 🕔 Mon–Sat 2pm–1:30am

THE OASES
Abduh's (£)

Well-established restaurant serving simple Egyptian dishes, breakfast and fresh juices on a terrace where you tend to meet everyone else in town.

✉ Central market square, Siwa Town ☎ 046-460 1243
🕔 8am–midnight

Al Babinshal Restaurant (£–££)

On the atmospheric roof terrace of the hotel, in the old abandoned town of Shali, this restaurant serves up a romantic candlelit Egyptian dinner.

✉ Al Babinshal hotel; Siwa Town ☎ 046-460 1499

🕐 5pm–11pm

Popular Restaurant (£)

Better known as Bayyoumi's, this eatery serves meat and vegetable stews, bread, omelettes and cold beer, but check the price first.

✉ At the main intersection of Al Bawiti, Bahariya

🕐 5:30am–10pm

Restaurant of Al Badawiyya Hotel (£–££)

Excellent restaurant with well-prepared, freshly cooked Egyptian food served in a courtyard.

✉ Farafra ☎ 092-751 0060 🕐 All day

Tanta Waa Cafeteria & Restaurant (£–££)

See page 59.

SHOPPING

HANDICRAFTS

Ganoub Traditional Crafts

Lovely little shop that sells the best of the oases crafts, including the typical camel-wool blankets and rugs, as well as a small selection of books on the oases and postcards.

✉ Shari' Misr, Al Bawiti, Bahariya

Girl's Work Shop

Great store selling only beautiful crafts made by girls and women in Bahariya oasis, providing them with some welcome income and the power that comes with that. Look out for the embroideries and great socks.

✉ Just south of Shari' Misr, Al Bawiti, Bahariya ☎ No phone 🕐 Sat–Thu 10am–1pm

Naglaa Sonusy

This painter, whose works reflect life in the oasis, sells from a room near her house on the road to the Al Beshmo spring in Al Bawiti.
☎ 012-429 5299

Siwa Traditional Handicraft

An excellent selection of some of the best crafts in Siwa, some embroidered by the owner Ali Abdallah's wife.
✉ Central market square, Siwa Town ☎ 010-304 1191

ENTERTAINMENT

Alexandria Centre of Arts

Great cultural centre in a white-washed villa, with contemporary art exhibitions, free concerts, library and cinema.
✉ 1 Tariq al Hurreya, Alexandria ☎ 03-495 6633

Alexandria Opera House

Beautifully restored opera house hosting regular performances of opera, theatre and ballet.
✉ 22 Tariq al Hurreya, opposite Cinema Royale, Alexandria ☎ 03-486 5106; www.cairoopera.org

Bibliotheca Alexandrina

Most important cultural venue, with international musical and dance performances, as well as major exhibitions (➤ 119).
✉ Corniche al Bahr, Chatby, Alexandria ☎ 03-483 9999; www.bibalex.org

SPORTS AND ACTIVITIES

Desert Driving

A desert safari is an unforgettable experience, but it needs care and advance preparation, as well as an experienced guide. One of the best is Peter Gaballa, who runs the excellent Egypt Off Road company (www.egyptoffroad.com; tel: 010-147 5462). He organizes longer trips in the desert, and teaches newcomers how to drive in the desert. Other experienced guides include Hisham Nessim (tel: 012-780 7999; www.raid4x4egypt .com) and Khalifa Expedition (tel: 012-321 5445; www.khalifaexp.com).

The Nile Valley and Lake Nasser

In a land with little rain, ancient Egyptians recognized that the Nile's annual summer flooding was a blessing, and so organized themselves to make the most of the flood and the fertile silt the river left as it receded. In the process they created the model for society as we know it; a hierarchy of workers, administrators and higher management (pharaohs) that also made possible the construction of huge temples and tombs.

Aswan

Buhayrat Nasir

The annual flooding created seasons of field work and enforced rest, which characterized life in the Egyptian countryside until the end of the 19th century. The completion of the two Aswan dams (1902 and 1965), which lost Nubia beneath Lake Nasser, ended that annual cycle of drought and flood. In spite of the many changes that have followed, the Nile remains as much Egypt's lifeline as it was in the past.

LUXOR

The modern city of Luxor covers part of ancient Thebes, also
known as Waset or Apet. One of the great cities of the ancient
world, Thebes spread across both sides of the Nile and was the
political capital of Egypt during the Middle and New Kingdoms.
Some of the most famous pharaohs – Ramses II, Tutankhamun,
Hatshepsut, Seti I – left their mark here. Long after political power
passed to the north, Theban temples remained the centre of
religious influence. The glory of Thebes was still very real when
the Greek poet Homer wrote about its 100 gates, but the sixth-
century-BC Persian King Cambyses hastened its decline by setting
fire to everything that could be burned. Most of what has survived
that and the ravages of the centuries are the remains of stone
temples and rock-cut tombs.

Early Christians defaced many temple images and converted
some of the courts into churches, while Arab Muslims, whose

religion banned the representation of people, generally showed no interest in the ruins. Difficulties of Nile travel gave Thebes and the rest of the Upper Nile Valley a legendary status in the West. Its rediscovery, starting in earnest in the 18th century and continuing today (KV5, the largest tomb so far found in Egypt, is the latest to be excavated in the Valley of the Kings) has attracted many visitors from around the world. At the time of writing, Luxor is undergoing a major face-lift making it into a modern city, with attractive streets, a gorgeous station and a paved souk. Great effort is going into cleaning and clearing the monuments as much as possible, to protect them and to make Luxor the largest open-air museum in the world.

✚ 16M

LUXOR'S EAST BANK

Karnak

Best places to see, ➤ 44–45.

Ma'bad al Uqsur (Luxor Temple)

The Temple of Luxor or the "*harem* of the south", like nearby Karnak, is dedicated to the Theban triad of Amun-Min, Mut and Khonsu, but it is a far more coherent building than Karnak as fewer pharaohs have made additions. During the *Opet* (fertility) festival, a procession of holy barges brought Amun's statue from Karnak to Luxor Temple, where he was united with his wife Mut to ensure an excellent harvest. The two temples are connected by a long avenue, lined with sphinxes, which is now being excavated. The mosque built over part of the temple is dedicated to Luxor's patron saint Abu al Haggag, during whose *moulid* (➤ 24) feluccas are pulled around the temple.

The First Pylon, built by Ramses II, features his favourite theme of victory at the battle of Kadesh. His two colossi, a ruined standing statue and one of two splendid obelisks (the other one now adorns the Place de la Concorde in Paris) flank the entrance. In the Court of Ramses II there is an interesting relief of the temple itself and, to the right, a funerary procession led by Ramses II's many sons. Beyond the Second Pylon the impressive Colonnade of Amenhotep III leads to the wide Court of Amenhotep III and a small Hypostyle Hall. The inner sanctum contains a number of shrines, including a columned portico used as a chapel by Roman soldiers, Alexander the Great's Sanctuary of the Sacred Barge and, to the left, Amenhotep III's Birth Room, near which the cache of statues now on view in the Luxor Museum (➤ 144) were found.

✉ Corniche 🕐 Daily 6am–10pm in summer, 6am–9pm in winter (best explored in daylight, but try to return at night when spotlights add to the atmosphere and accentuate the carvings) 👣 Moderate

Mathaf al Mumia (Mummification Museum)

Luxor's mummification museum, the first of its kind in the world, houses a unique collection of mummies, including mummified animals such as cats, fish and crocodiles, as well as tools used for mummification. Everything is well displayed and labelled, giving a clear insight into the whole mummification process.

✉ Corniche ☎ 095-238 1501 🕓 May–Sep daily 9–1, 4–10; Oct–Apr 9–1, 4–9 🖐 Moderate

Mathaf al Uqsur li l Athaar (Luxor Museum)

The small modern Luxor Museum is one of the finest in Egypt and most exhibits are from local temples and tombs. What sets it apart is that displays are carefully chosen, well-labelled and perfectly lit, to make the most of their beauty. Much of the ground floor is dedicated to New Kingdom statues, including a superb bust of the young Tuthmosis III (No. 61) and a bizarre alabaster statue of the crocodile god Sobek holding Amenhotep III (No. 107). A separate gallery is dedicated to the glory of Thebes, highlighting its military and technological skills.

The upper floor has a mural from Akhenaten's temple at Karnak, with the king and his wife worshipping the sun god Aten. A glass case shows some objects from Tutankhamun's tomb in the Valley of the Kings (➤ 40–41), including two fine model boats, a superb gold-inlaid cow's head, sandals and arrows. The New Hall displays the cache of 26 statues found in 1989, near Amenhotep III's Birth Room in Luxor Temple.

✉ Corniche ☎ 095-238 0269 🕓 May–Sep daily 9–1, 5–10, Oct–Apr 9–1, 4–9 🖐 Moderate; additional ticket (inexpensive) for New Hall

LUXOR'S WEST BANK

Biban al Harim (Valley of the Queens)

Known in ancient times as the "place of beauty", this was the resting place of more than 80 queens and princes from the 18th to the 20th Dynasties (1570–1070BC), many of whom have not been identified.

The tombs in this valley are far less grand and elaborate than those in the Valley of the Kings, and many were left unfinished, suggesting that queens and their offspring were considerably less important than the pharaohs themselves. The tomb of Nefertari, the wife of Ramses II, is the exception, and its exquisite paintings have been restored. Several sons of Ramses III died in childhood of smallpox and, unusually, the reliefs in their tombs show them being led by their father through the underworld.

✉ 3km (2 miles) south of the Valley of the Nobles 🕐 May–Sep daily 6–6; Oct–Apr 6–5 ✋ Moderate ❓ The Tomb of Nefertari is closed at the time of writing, and it's unclear if it will open again in the near future

Biban al Muluk (Valley of the Kings)
Best places to see, ➤ 40–41.

Biban al Nubalaa (Tombs of the Nobles)
While the pharaohs' tombs were decorated with religious texts,
the tombs of the nobles depict the good life they had led on earth
in the hope that it would continue after their death. The result is
often more satisfying than the royal tombs. It is easy to imagine
these people's lives and interests, because their tombs show
scenes of family life, agriculture, and how they imagined the
afterlife, including the boat journey to Abydos and funerary
banquets. As the quality of limestone was too poor for carvings,
these scenes were painted on plaster. Three groups of tombs are
particularly worth visiting for their amazing and well-preserved
paintings: Nakht and Menna; Rekhmire and Sennofer; Ramose,
Userhat and Khaemhat.

✉ West Bank 🕐 Daily 6–5 💲 Moderate per group of tombs (tickets
available from Antiquities Inspectorate office)

Deir al Bahari (Mortuary Temple of Hatshepsut)

Dramatically set against the Theban hills, this splendid mortuary temple built by Queen Hatshepsut's architect (and perhaps also her lover), Senenmut, always surprises with its simplicity. Queen Hatshepsut was one of the few female pharaohs to reign over Egypt, taking power from her stepson, Tuthmosis III, when her husband Tuthmosis II died. The temple terraces were filled with trees and fountains, and linked to the Nile by an avenue of Sphinxes. The colonnades of the Lower Terrace were defaced by Tuthmosis III (now closed for restoration), but the Middle Terrace colonnades are fascinating with the Birth Colonnade, confirming the Queen's divine parentage, and the Punt Colonnade, depicting her journey to Punt (probably in today's Somalia). Beyond lies the Chapel of Hathor with bovine Hathor columns. The restored Higher Terrace has the Sanctuary of Amun hewn into the rock.

✉ West Bank ⏰ Daily 6–5 🖐 Moderate ❓ It is possible to walk over the hill, or take a donkey, to the Valley of the Kings (➤ 40–41) with fantastic views over Luxor and the monuments

Deir al Medina (Workers' Village)

Artists and artisans worked on tombs in the Valley of the Kings (➤ 40–41) for ten days at a time before returning to their family home in Deir al Medina, where they built their own tombs. The tomb of Sennedjem has very fine wall-paintings of agricultural scenes, Sennedjem and his wife in front of the gods, and a depiction of the tree of life, from which a goddess appears. The tomb of Ankherha is equally brightly painted with scenes of Ankherha's family with lots of children. Further up the slope is the tomb of Peshedu, with a beautiful scene in the burial chamber.

✉ West Bank ⏰ Daily 6–5 🖐 Moderate (tickets available from Antiquities Inspectorate office)

Howard Carter House

On a hill on the road to the Valley of the Kings stands the domed house of the famous British archaeologist Howard Carter, where he lived during his search and excavation of Tutankhamun's tomb (➤ 41). The mud-brick house has been restored and displays tools Carter used in excavations and a collection of photographs of work under way. A cafe-terrace should open soon, which will make it a very pleasant stop on the way to the Valley of the Kings.

✉ West Bank 🕐 Daily 6–5 ✋ Free

Ma'bad Seti (Temple of Seti I)

Dedicated to the god Amun and to Seti's father Ramses I, this largely destroyed temple still shows the hallmark of Seti I (1291–1278BC) with some of the finest wall decorations and reliefs of the New Kingdom. The first two pylons and courts have disappeared and today only the temple proper remains. A colonnade leads into a Hypostyle Hall, with columns decorated with reliefs of Seti I and Ramses I making offerings to the gods. The chapel to the left of the temple's main entrance is dedicated to Ramses I, who died before a temple could be built for him. Few tourists come here, which adds to the pleasure of visiting it.

✉ Gurna 🕐 Daily 6–5 ✋ Moderate (tickets available from Antiquities Inspectorate office)

MadinAt Habu (Mortuary Temple of Ramses III)

Ramses III (1182–1151BC) modelled this impressive temple on his forefather Ramses II's mortuary temple (Ramesseum, ➤ 150). Madinat Habu is not on many tourists' itinerary, even though it was the last classical pharaonic temple built, with very few later additions. The vast temple complex is entered through a high gatehouse, built as a Syrian-style fortress, and the steps lead to the pharaoh's pleasure apartments with a good view over the grounds. The magnificent First Pylon records battles that Ramses III never fought, most likely copied from Ramses II's temple. The

First and Second Courts are vast and lined with images of Ramses III making offerings to the gods, but the Hypostyle Hall and Inner Sanctuaries were severely damaged during an earthquake in 27BC. Take a walk along the outer walls, decorated with more giant reliefs of Ramses III fishing, hunting or at war.

✉ Kom Lolah 🕐 Daily 6–5
✋ Moderate (tickets available from Antiquities Inspectorate office)
🍴 Two cafes outside the gates serve lunch (£)

Memnon Colossi

Amenhotep III's (1386–1349BC) giant colossi overlook green fields – their faces, as well as the mortuary temple they guarded, disappeared long ago. A crack in one of the statues led the Greeks to believe this was Memnon singing to Eos, hence the name; it was repaired in AD199. Smaller statues of Queen Tiy and Amenhotep III's mother, Mutemuia, flank the pharaoh's legs and the sides of the seats are decorated with sunken reliefs of round-bellied Nile gods with papyrus and lotus flowers.

Ramesseum

Ramses II (1279–1212BC) built magnificent temples, including large parts of Karnak (➤ 44–45) and Luxor Temple (➤ 142) and two temples at Abu Simbel, but his own mortuary temple fell. The temple entrance leads to the First Pylon, decorated with scenes from the Battle at Kadesh. Near the Second Pylon is the base of the statue of "Ozymandias" (a Greek misreading of one of Ramses's titles), which inspired the British poet Shelley. Once the largest statue in the world, weighing over 900 tonnes, the head and part of the torso remain where they landed; other parts are now in museums all over the world. The Hypostyle Hall is decorated with battle scenes, and the ceiling of the Astronomic Room is painted with the oldest known 12-month calendar.

✉ Opposite the Tombs of the Nobles 🕐 May–Sep daily 6–6; Oct–May 6–5 💷 Moderate (tickets available from Antiquities Inspectorate office)

The Central Nile Valley

This area may be subject to security alerts (➤ 32, Personal Safety).

ABYDOS
Best places to see, ➤ 36–37.

BENI HASAN
Beni Hasan is a Middle Kingdom necropolis on the east bank of the river, with four tombs open to the public. They belonged to local governors and are remarkable for their elegant columns and fine paintings on stucco. These depict scenes from daily life, agriculture and hunting, as well as more unusual acrobats and wrestlers.

➕ 13H ✉ 20km (12.5 miles) south of Al Minya ⊗ Daily 8–5 ✋ Moderate 🚗 Private taxi from Al Minya, ferry across

DANDARA, TEMPLE OF HATHOR
The beautiful Temple of Hathor was built between 125BC and AD60 as part of an attempt by the Ptolemies and the Romans to reinforce their position by claiming association with the ancient Egyptian gods. There was probably an earlier temple of Hathor here, as this was the site where Hathor was believed to have given birth to Horus' son. During the New Year festival, Hathor's statue was taken in procession to the roof, where it was exposed to the sun god Re before being escorted to the temple at Edfu (➤ 158) to be reunited with Horus. Scenes of this festival decorate the temple walls, as well as reliefs of Roman emperors performing ancient Egyptian rituals. The carvings are much cruder than earlier pharaonic work, but the temple has been well-preserved and remains impressive.

➕ 16L ✉ 4km (2.5 miles) across the Nile from Qena, 64km (40 miles) north of Luxor ⊗ Daily 7–6 ✋ Inexpensive 🍴 Cafe (£) 🚂 Train to Qena, then taxi. ❓ Private taxi, cruise boat or organized tour from Luxor

AL MINYA

The provincial town of Al Minya was a good base for visiting the surrounding antiquities until the 1990s when it became a hothouse for Islamic militants. Things have calmed down and it is again a pleasant place to be, but the police presence has remained. The town has a few dilapidated colonial buildings and an interesting Muslim and Coptic cemetery, Zawiyet al Mayyetin, on the West Bank, to which the dead were transported on feluccas until not long ago.

🚩 13G ✉ 245km (152 miles) south of Cairo 🚆 Trains from Cairo and Luxor
ℹ Governorate Building, Corniche al Nil, Luxor; tel: 086-236 0150

SOHAG

Sohag is a large town with a large Coptic community. Its main attractions are the nearby monasteries on the edge of the desert. Deir al Abyad (White Monastery), founded in the fourth century by St Shenuda, looks like a pharaonic temple. Once it was a thriving community of more than 2,000 monks, but only a few remain today. The smaller Deir al Ahmar (Red Monastery) was founded by St Bishoi, a disciple of St Shenuda. The Sohag Museum is expected to open in 2012, and will display local antiquities.

🚩 14K ✉ 206km (128 miles) south of Al Minya, 472km (293 miles) south of Cairo ⏰ White: Mon 7am–sunset; Red: Mon 7am–midnight 🚆 Trains from Cairo, Asyut, Al Minya and Luxor; monasteries reached by taxi only

TELL AL AMARNA

The fascinating city founded by the rebellious pharaoh Akhenaten (1350–1334BC) and his beautiful wife Nefertiti was abandoned after 14 years, when the king died and the priests from Karnak destroyed it. They had left Thebes to establish Akhetaten, their new capital, dedicated to the sun god Aten. The Royal Road passes the ruins of the Great Temple of Aten, the Royal Residence, the State Palace and the Sanctuary of Aten. On the other side of the landing post are the better preserved Temple of

Nefertiti and the Northern Tombs of Amarna nobles, with scenes representing the joyful life at the capital. The Southern Tombs are the finest, especially those of Mahu and Ay.

🕂 13H ✉ 60km (37 miles) south of Al Minya ☀ Daily 8–5 in summer; 8–4 in winter ✋ Inexpensive, plus extra ticket for royal tombs ❓ The site is vast so you will need a private car or taxi to get around. No electricity in some tombs, bring a torch

TUNA AL GEBEL

Only a small area of the vast necropolis is open to the public. Near the entrance is the Sacred Animal Necropolis for mummified baboons, ibises and other animals. Further south is the City of the Dead, where the tomb of High Priest Petosiris (300BC) has fine wall-paintings of agriculture, crafts and funerary processions.

🕂 13H ✉ 50km (31 miles) south of Al Minya ☀ Daily 8–5 ✋ Inexpensive 🚗 Private taxi only

Southern Nile Valley

ASWAN

Aswan, Egypt's southernmost town, feels more like Africa than the rest of Egypt. The people, mostly Nubians, are taller and darker than Upper Egyptians, their music and culture has more in common with the Sudan than with Cairo or Alexandria, and the air smells sweet and tropical. Two deserts, the Eastern Desert and the Sahara, close in on the Nile, which here flows around a series of granite rocks and islands. The First Cataract, which ancient Egyptians believed was the source of the Nile, once marked the end of the civilized world, as boats were unable to pass this barrier. Yebu, on Elephantine Island, was the Old Kingdom frontier, as well as an important cult centre. Today, as in ancient times, Aswan is renowned for its wonderful winter climate and beautiful setting.

✚ 160

Aga Khan Mausoleum

This small but dignified mausoleum was built for Mohammed Shah Aga Khan (1877–1957), the leader of the Ismailis, a Shi'ite Muslim sect. The Aga Khan, famous for his incredible wealth, fell in love with this spot and with Aswan. His widow, Omme Habibeh, popularly known as "The Begum", used to spend her winters in the villa below the mausoleum, but since her death in 2000 she lies buried beside him. The views over the Nile and Aswan are spectacular, especially at sunset.

✉ West Bank of the Nile ⏰ Closed to the public 🚤 Felucca, no public ferries

Mathaf al Athaar (Aswan Antiquities Museum)

Housed in the villa of Sir William Willcocks, the British engineer who designed the old Aswan dam, the museum has a massive collection of objects found on Elephantine Island and a collection of artefacts salvaged from the flooded areas beyond the dam. The museum itself is rather dusty, but the annexe arranged by the Swiss-German mission in the late 1990s is interesting and well arranged. Exhibits give an insight into everyday life in ancient Egypt – weaving, trade, religion, hunting and farming.

Look for the superb gold-covered statue of the sacred ram, a representation of the god Khnum.

By the Nile is the Nilometer, with Greek, Roman, pharaonic and Arabic numerals. It was a very important instrument, as taxes were calculated according to the height of the Nile. Further south are the ruins of ancient Yebu. Beyond a gateway, on which Alexander II is shown worshipping Khnum, are the ruins of a 30th Dynasty Temple of Khnum. Although this site is still being excavated, it is worth a visit for the spectacular views of Aswan and the Nile.

✉ On tip of Elephantine Island
🕓 May–Sep daily 8:30–6; Oct–Apr 8–5 ✋ Inexpensive, includes visit to the Nilometer and ruins of Yebu
⛴ Ferry from the landing dock near EgyptAir office

Mathaf al Nuba (Nubia Museum)

The Nubia Museum is a tribute to the Nubian people, whose lands were flooded after the construction of the Aswan Dam. In a beautiful modern building vaguely inspired by traditional Nubian architecture, the museum's well-displayed, well-labelled exhibits follow the history, art and culture of Nubia from prehistoric times (*c* 4500BC) to the present day. Among the highlights are the oldest skeleton found in the Toshka region, a superb statue of a 25th Dynasty Kushite priest of Amun and an interesting display explaining the development of irrigation along the Nile. There is a reconstructed Nubian house in the museum garden, and a cave with prehistoric rock carvings of animals.

✉ Shari' Abtal al Tahrir ☎ 097-231 9111 🕑 Daily 9–1, 5–9
✋ Moderate ❓ No photography

Al Mesalla al Naqsa (Unfinished Obelisk)

This might have been the largest obelisk ever, 41m (134ft) high and weighing almost 1,200 tonnes, but it was left unfinished in the quarry when a flaw in the granite was discovered. It was meant to be one of a pair, the other of which is the Lateran Obelisk, once erected in the Temple of Tuthmosis III in Karnak but now in Rome.

✉ 1.5km (1 mile) south of Aswan on the road to Philae
🕑 Daily 7–4 (8–6 in summer) ✋ Moderate

Philae Temples
Best places to see, ➤ 52–53.

Al Sadd al Ali (High Dam)
The old Aswan dam, completed by the British in 1902, was soon found to be too small, but it wasn't until the 1960s that a new dam was built. President Nasser saw the High Dam as the key to making Egypt self-reliant, as controlling the Nile flood would provide electricity for the whole country. The High Dam is immense: 111m (364ft) high, more than 3.8km (2.3 miles) long, 980m (3,215ft) wide at the base, 40m (130ft) at the top with a volume some 17 times that of the Pyramid of Khufu. Lake Nasser, the world's largest reservoir, at over 6,000sq km (2,316sq miles), has saved Egypt from famine and floods several times, and made it possible to irrigate vast stretches of desert. But it isn't all good news. As a result of the dam Nubians lost their land, ancient monuments were inundated by the lake (some were rescued by a UNESCO salvage operation), Nile silt no longer fertilizes Egyptian fields and the ground-water level has risen, threatening monuments all along the Nile in Egypt.

✉ 7km (4 miles) south of the old Aswan dam
🚾 Inexpensive ❓ Photography of the dam is strictly forbidden, passport may be required

Southern Nile Valley

DARAW

The only reason people stop at Daraw is to visit its large camel market. Camels are brought across the desert along the Forty Days Road from Darfur and Kordofan in Sudan, to a place north of Abu Simbel. From there they are driven to Daraw and sometimes to Birqash near Cairo. The market is a fascinating place, especially in the early morning, when Sudanese traders in their traditional costumes prefer to do their business.

🚩 16P ✉ 40km (25 miles) north of Aswan ⭐ Camel market: every day before noon, but Sun morning is best, with the most camels ❓ Private minibus or taxi from Aswan to Kom Ombo

EDFU (TEMPLE OF HORUS)

After Karnak (➤ 44–45), this is the largest temple in Egypt and the best-preserved, having been buried in the sand and built over with houses until archaeologists uncovered it in the 1860s. Begun in 237BC by Ptolemy III and dedicated to the falcon god Horus, the temple stands on the site where Horus is believed to have fought his uncle Seth for control of the world. Much has been learned about this temple from building and foundation texts inscribed on the walls.

The entrance is past a row of bazaars, and the path leads to the 36m-high (118ft) Pylon fronted by two huge falcon statues of Horus. On the outside walls of the temple complex Neos Dionysos, Ptolemy XII is shown slaughtering his enemies. Behind the pylon is the Great Court, where the reliefs depict the annual Festival of the

Beautiful Meeting, when Horus' statue was taken to Hathor's
temple at Dandara (➤ 151). Another black granite statue of Horus
flanks the outer hypostyle hall, followed by the smaller inner
hypostyle hall at the back of which is a wall with all the recipes for
perfumes and potions needed in the temple. At the back of the
temple is the Sanctuary of Horus, which still contains the granite
altar on which rested Horus' sacred boat, and the large granite
shrine, which the statue of the god once inhabited.

🚹 16N ✉ 115km (71 miles) south of Luxor, 105km (65 miles) north of Aswan
🕒 May–Sep daily 7am–10pm; Oct–Apr 7am–9pm 🎫 Moderate 🍴 Cafe (£)
❓ Private taxi or tour

ESNA TEMPLE

The temple of the ram-headed god Khnum was probably as large as Edfu after the reconstruction by Ptolemy VI (*c*180BC), but most of it remains hidden under the village. Only the Hypostyle Hall, a first-century AD addition by the Roman emperor Claudius, has been excavated. Its 24 painted columns with capitals in the shape of different flowers and plants form an enclosed garden, while Roman emperors adorn the walls, making offerings to the Egyptian deities.

✚ 15N ✉ 54km (33 miles) south of Luxor, 155km (96 miles) north of Aswan
🕓 May–Sep daily 6–6; Oct–Apr 6–5 ✋ Inexpensive ❓ Private taxi or tour

KOM OMBO TEMPLE

Most Egyptian temples were dedicated to a single deity, but Kom Ombo Temple, started by Ptolemy VI (*c*180 BC) and finished by Roman emperor Augustus (30BC–AD14), was dedicated to two: Horus the Elder and Sobek. The eastern side was devoted to the crocodile god Sobek, and the Chapel of Hathor near the entrance housed some mummified crocodiles. The other side of the temple was dedicated to Horus the Elder, known as the "Good Doctor", and attracted sick pilgrims, who took part in complicated rituals here in the hope of a cure. The temple's dramatic location, on a bend in the river, was also its undoing – much of the pylon and the forecourt were swept away by the Nile, though a double entrance to the inner Hypostyle Hall survives with elegant floral columns. Behind the two sanctuaries there are seven chapels on whose outer walls is depicted an interesting display of medical instruments, clear evidence that ancient Egyptian surgeons performed highly sophisticated operations.

✚ 16P ✉ 170km (105 miles) south of Luxor, 45km (28 miles) north of Aswan 🕐 May–Sep daily 7am–9pm; Oct–Apr 7–8 ✋ Moderate 🍴 Cafeteria (£) ❓ Private taxi or tour

Lake Nasser

UNESCO relocated many Nubian temples threatened by the building of the High Dam and the creation of Lake Nasser. For many years, fishing boats and the occasional ferry to Sudan had the lake to themselves, but several cruise ships now operate between Aswan and Abu Simbel, fishing trips are increasingly popular and several luxury hotels are planned.

ABU SIMBEL

The two temples at Abu Simbel were built by Ramses II and are the most spectacular Nubian monuments. The facade of the Great Temple of Re-Harakhte is dominated by four magnificent seated colossi of Ramses II, cut into the cliff, flanked by other members of the royal family. The Hypostyle Hall, lined with 10m-high (33ft) Osirid statues of the pharaoh, is decorated with superb reliefs of his famous victories. The temples were hand-sawn out of the rock-face, cut into 1,050 blocks and reconstructed on an artificial hill. Near by is the smaller Temple of Hathor, fronted by statues of Ramses II and his favourite wife, Nefertari, with their children. The Hypostyle Hall, supported by Hathor-headed columns, has reliefs of the queen watching her husband at war. A cow statue of Hathor in the sanctuary is decorated with reliefs of Nefertari and Ramses.

✚ 14T ✉ 280km (174 miles) south of Aswan 🕐 Daily 6am–6pm summer; 6–5 in winter, or until the last plane leaves 🖐 Expensive 🍴 Cafe (£) 🚌 Buses or private taxis from Aswan ✈ From Cairo and Aswan; return tickets include transfers between airport and site. If outgoing plane is delayed there may be little time at site ❓ Sound and light show, tel: 097-231 2811; www.soundandlight.com.eg; expensive). On 22 Feb and 22 Oct at dawn the sun rays touch the cult statue

AMADA

The oldest Egyptian temple in Nubia, Amada was built by Tuthmosis III and Amenhotep II, dedicated to Amun-Re and Re-Harakhte. Reliefs in the inner right-hand chapel show the temple's foundation rituals. In the sand lie early drawings of animals (including elephants) carved on stone. Close by is the Rock Temple of al Derr, built by Ramses II, with excellent colourful reliefs, and the rock-cut Tomb of Penne, viceroy of Nubia under Ramses VI, with traditional themes decorating the walls.

✚ 15S ✉ 170km (105 miles) south of the High Dam 🕐 Daily 6–6 🖐 Moderate 🚢 Cruise boat only

KALABSHA

Built during the great 18th Dynasty
(1570–1293BC) and rebuilt under the
Ptolemies and Romans, Kalabsha was dedicated to the Nubian
fertility god Marul. Much of its later decorations have survived.
The monuments were relocated here from other sites in Nubia
when Lake Nasser was formed and the Roman Kiosk of Qertassi
originally stood 10km (6 miles) away. More interesting is Beit al
Wali (the Governor's House), a small rock-hewn temple built by
the Governor of Kush (Ethiopia) during the reign of Ramses II.

🚹 16Q ✉ Next to the High Dam ⏰ Daily 8–5 🖐 Moderate ❓ Taxi from
Aswan. Temple itself can often only be reached by boat from the harbour

QASR IBRIM (QASR FORTRESS)

Qasr Ibrim remains where it was founded in around 1000BC, but
what was formerly a mountain top dominating the Nile now only
just manages to stay above Lake Nasser. Remains of a healing
centre, dedicated to Isis, are visible, as are walls of a 10th-century
Christian basilica. From the Ottoman invasion in 1517 until 1812
the castle was manned by Bosnian soldiers.

🚹 15S ✉ 40km (25 miles) north of Abu Simbel ⏰ Daily 6–6 🖐 Free
🚢 Cruise boat only

WADI AL SEBU'A (VALLEY OF THE LIONS)

The Valley of the Lions was named after the 16 sphinxes lining the
entrance. The highlights are the statues and images of Ramses II,
in whose reign it was built, and decorations from the time of early
Christians. The Temple of Dakka, reconstructed nearby, was begun
by Arkamani, a Meroite king contemporary with Ptolemy II
(285–246BC). Dedicated to Thoth, it is the only Egyptian temple
facing north. Also here are the remains of the Roman temple of
Maharraka, dedicated to Isis and Serapis.

🚹 15S ✉ 135km (84 miles) south of the High Dam ⏰ Daily 6–6
🖐 Moderate 🚢 Cruise boat only

HOTELS

ABU SIMBEL
Eskaleh (£–££)

Charming small guest house and Nubian cultural centre, run by the Nubian musician and guide Fikri Kachif. The large house has five spacious rooms with air-conditioning, fan and tiled bathrooms, a library on Nubian history and culture and several sitting areas. Fikri grows his own vegetables in the large garden overlooking Lake Nasser – his foamy *karkadeh* (hibiscus drink) is the best in Egypt. The restaurant serves three-course meals with grilled meat or fish fresh from the lake.

✉ Entrance of Abu Simbel, past the bridge to the left ☎ 012-368 0521/097-340 1288

ASWAN
Beit al Kerem (££)

This is a small modern hotel at the foot of the Tomb of the Nobles, in a Nubian village on Aswan's West Bank. The hotel has calm, large rooms decorated with local furnishings, very friendly staff and a good rooftop restaurant.

✉ Gharb Aswan, Aswan West Bank ☎ 019-239 9443; www.betelkerem.com

Keylany (£)

Best budget hotel in town with spotless, air-conditioned rooms with bathrooms and very friendly and helpful staff. The hotel also has a pleasant roof terrace with sun loungers, an excellent internet cafe and a good travel agency for tours in and out of Aswan.

✉ 25 Shari' Keylani ☎ 097-231 7337; www.keylanyhotel.com

Marhaba Palace (££)

The mock-pharaonic facade hides small but comfortable rooms with good private bathrooms, air-conditioning and satellite TV. The rooftop terrace commands great views over the Nile and the small park in front of the hotel. The hotel has a good pool, very friendly staff and an ultra-central location.

✉ Off the Corniche, near Midan al Mahatta ☎ 097-233 0102

Nile Hotel (££)

Great mid-range hotel in a central location with views of the Nile. Well-kept rooms and staff are helpful.

✉ Corniche an Nil ☎ 097-231 4222; www.nilehotel-aswan.com

Nuba Nile (£)

Like the Keylany (▶ 165), this is another good budget option near the train station, with tidy rooms, some with private bathrooms and air-conditioning. There is a good internet cafe in the building.

✉ Just off Midan al Mahatta ☎ 097-231 3267

Sofitel Old Cataract (£££)

This grand hotel, which was immortalized in the film of Agatha Christie's *Death on the Nile*, was opened in 1899 and is probably Egypt's most famous hotel. This splendid Moorish building is filled to the brim with nostalgia, and its beautiful rooms command wonderful views over the Nile and Elephantine Island. Tea on the terrace at sunset is a must. The hotel is due to reopen in late 2011 after a complete renovation.

✉ Shari' Abtal al Tahrir ☎ 097-231 6000; www.sofitel.com

LUXOR
Amon (£)

A family-run hotel set amid fields, with very clean rooms (with and without private bathrooms), a roof terrace with marvellous views of the West Bank and a lovely tropical garden where breakfast is served. Book in advance.

✉ Geziret al Bairat, West Bank (near the ferry landing, left at the Mobil petrol station) ☎ 095-231 0912

Beit Sabée (£–££)

This simple but gorgeous hotel has featured in interior-design magazines, for its use of bright Nubian colours and local textiles. A home away from home that happens to overlook the temple of Ramses III at Medinet Habu.

✉ Kom Lolah, West Bank ☎ 010-632 4926; www.beitsabee.com

Al Moudira (£££)

Spectacular and luxurious hotel built in local style, on the edge of the desert. The rooms are vast and beautifully decorated with locally made furniture and antiques. The pool is set in the gardens that overlook the Thebes mountains.

✉ Daba'iyya, 15km (9 miles) south of the ticket office ☎ 012-325 1307; www.moudira.com

Nour al Qurna (£)

Beautiful small hotel with large, simply but tastefully decorated rooms with local handmade furniture, ceiling fans, mosquito nets and a view over the sugarcane fields.

✉ Opposite the ticket office, Gurna ☎ 095-311 430

Old Winter Palace (£££)

Grand colonial hotel with large rooms, stylishly decorated, overlooking either the Nile and the Theban hills or, at the back, the lush, very well groomed gardens. There is a superb large swimming pool in the gardens, and several excellent restaurants.

✉ Shari' Corniche al Nil, West Bank ☎ 095-380 422; www.sofitel.com

RESTAURANTS

ASWAN
Aswan Panorama (£)

Waterfront cafe-restaurant serving simple Egyptian *mezze* (appetizers) and other dishes, as well as drinks and fresh juices. For those who want something quieter than the lively atmosphere at the Emy or the Aswan Moon.

✉ Corniche al Nil, beside the Aswan Moon ☎ 097-231 6169 🕐 All day

Emy (£)

Cafe-restaurant on a boat moored on the river bank. The Emy is popular with felucca captains so it is a good place to look if you want to rent a felucca. One of the few places to sell beer, there are also fresh juices, sandwiches and Egyptian dishes.

✉ Next to Aswan Moon (▶ 58), Corniche al Nil ☎ 097-230 4349 🕐 Daily 9am–midnight

Nubian Beach (£)

Delightful Nubian cafe-restaurant set right on the Nile against a giant sand dune. Good Egyptian and Nubian stews, grills and salads, or just a place for an afternoon tea.

✉ West Bank, past Aga Khan Mausoleum, only reached by boat ☎ No phone ⏰ Daily 10am–11pm

Old Cataract Terrace (££)

The view from this splendid hotel terrace is spectacular and Earl Grey tea with cakes and sandwiches is a treat, but it is expensive.

✉ Old Cataract Hotel, Shari' Abtal al Tahrir ☎ 097-316 000 ⏰ All day

Sunset (£–££)

This is a favourite with locals, who come to watch the sunset or who come with the family to eat pizza or grills. A great spot.

✉ Shari' Abtal et Tahrir, Nasr City ☎ 012-166 1480 ⏰ Daily 9am–3am

LUXOR

King's Head Pub (£–££)

A British pub with all the trimmings: darts, pub food, billiards, football on TV and popular with backpackers.

✉ Shari' Khaled Ibn al Walid ☎ 095-371 249 ⏰ 24 hours

La Mamma (££)

An Italian restaurant in a pleasant garden with a pond full of wading birds. The fresh pastas and meat dishes are good.

✉ Sheraton Hotel, Shari' Khalid Ibn Walid ☎ 095-237 4544 ⏰ Lunch, dinner

Maratonga Café-Restaurant (£)

This lovely shady terrace is a good place to stop for lunch or to see the late-afternoon sun shine orange on the magnificent temple. Serves simple but well-prepared Egyptian dishes.

✉ Opposite Madinat Habu Temple ⏰ All day

Maxime (££)

French-Egyptian restaurant that serves well-prepared traditional French bistro dishes, particularly reknowned in expat circles for its excellent steak-frites. The service is friendly and the wide menu offers good value. No alcohol.

✉ Shari' Khaled Ibn al Walid, between Isis and Sheraton Hotels, East Bank
☎ 095-238 6315 🕓 Daily 11.30am–midnight

Metropolitan Café (£–££)

Cafe-terrace down by the Nile, overlooking the river, serving cool beers, sunset cocktails, snacks and Egyptian and international cuisine. Good place to watch the sunset over the East Bank.

✉ Lower Level, Corniche al Nil, opposite Old Winter Palace, East Bank
☎ No phone 🕓 Daily 10am–11pm

Al Moudira (££–£££)

See page 59.

Oasis Café (£–££)

See page 59.

Restaurant Mohammed (£–££)

See page 59.

Es Sahaby Lane (£–££)

A friendly open-air restaurant and cafe, Es Sahaby Lane is in an alley off the souk and part of the Nefertiti Hotel. There's a large menu of snacks as well as good Egyptian dishes.

✉ Shari' as-Sahaby, off Shari' es Souq ☎ 095-236 5509;
www.nefertitihotel.com/sahabi.htm

Sofra (£–££)

See page 59.

Tutankhamun (£)

Tutankhamun is by far the best on this strip. The chef and owner used to cook in one of Luxor's five-star hotels. Chicken with rosemary, served with sweet Oriental rice, is a speciality.

✉ Near the public ferry landing on the West Bank ☎ 095-231 0918,
010-441 4478 🕓 All day

SHOPPING

BOOKSHOPS
Aboudi
Aboudi sells a huge range of books on Egypt in many languages including German, English, French, Spanish and Japanese, as well as a large selection of postcards and books for children on Egypt, the pharaohs and the pyramids.

✉ Tourist Bazaar, Corniche al Nil, next to the Winter Palace Hotel, Luxor
☎ 095-237 3390

HANDICRAFTS
Caravanserai
Beautifully painted shop selling interesting crafts mainly made by local women and women around the country. It is a friendly place where you'll want to spend some time.

✉ Kom Lolah, West Bank, Luxor ☎ 012-327 8771;
www.caravanserailuxor.com

Fair Trade Centre Luxor Outlet
This lovely shop sells handicrafts from non-governmental organization projects all over Egypt, and particularly from the nearby villages of Hegaza and Garagos. Very good selection and prices.

✉ Shari' al Karnak, Luxor ☎ 095-238 7015

Habiba
This tiny shop sells the best of Egyptian crafts, mostly fair trade, sourced from all over the country.

✉ Shari' Sidi Mahmoud, off the souq, Luxor ☎ 010-124 2026;
www.habiba.com

ENTERTAINMENT

Cocktail Sunset
A pontoon on the Nile, with two floors, this is as the name suggests the place to go at sunset or later at night for a cocktail or two, or ice-cold beer.

✉ Corniche al Nil, opposite Luxor Museum ☎ 095-238 0524

Suez Canal, Sinai and the Red Sea

Bûr Sa'îd
(Port Said)

Sinai

The Suez Canal divides Africa from Asia, and Sinai from the rest of Egypt. The desert was too savage for Nile dwellers to settle, but that didn't stop them visiting the mountains on both sides of the divide to find gold (around the Wadi Hammamat), turquoise (at the 12th Dynasty, 1990–1780BC, mines around Serabit al Khadem) and other minerals.

Sinai was always an important transit route and many passed through, from Moses and the Hebrews to Christian hermits living around Wadi Feiran and St Catherine's Monastery, and Muslim pilgrims, thousands of years later, making their way to Mecca. Apart from their traces, the region's main attraction is the sea and what lies beneath it. The days of pristine coastline are long gone, but there are still idyllic places in Sinai and along the Red Sea coast.

Suez Canal area

To reach the East from Europe before the 167km-long (103-mile) canal was built meant either sailing around Africa or crossing the desert between Cairo and Suez. When the canal opened in 1869, Suez enjoyed a boom and the new towns of Port Said and Ismailia were created. But the Arab-Israel conflict closed the canal, devastated the area (most of Suez was levelled and effectively abandoned between 1967 and 1973) and robbed the area of much of its wealth. Of the three, Port Said has recovered the best, helped by its tax-free status. Since it was nationalized in 1956, the canal has been one of Egypt's major sources of revenue.

ISMAILIA (ISMA'ILIYA)

The older, European-built quarter of the city retains its genteel air, typified by the Swiss-style house of Ferdinand de Lesseps, who dreamed and schemed the canal into existence. The dusty but interesting museum at Muhammed Ali Quay, built like a Ptolemaic

temple, has a good collection of Graeco-Roman and pharaonic artefacts. The city's other main attraction is its beaches, where you can watch freighters pass by.

🚩 8B ✉ 120km (75 miles) east of Cairo, 85km (53 miles) from Port Said
🍴 Cafes and restaurants (£–££) 🚌 Buses from Cairo, Hurghada, Port Said
ℹ 1st Floor, New Governate Building, Shari' Tugary; tel: 064-332 1078

PORT SAID (BUR SA'ID)

Port Said is no longer "the wickedest town in the East" – no more dirty postcards or canalside brothels – but it still attracts sailors from around the world. The sights are few: the canal itself – the most captivating thing to see; the plinth at the mouth of the canal where a statue of De Lesseps, the engineer, stood until blown up in 1956; and some grand belle époque buildings on the waterfront and around Shari' Memphis. The **Military Museum** has a small collection of antiquities and artefacts from the opening of the canal, including Khedive Ismail's carriage.

🚩 8A ✉ 225km (140 miles) from Cairo, 85km (53 miles) north of Ismailia
🍴 Cafes and restaurants (£–££) 🚌 Buses from Cairo, Suez, Ismailia, Hurghada ℹ 8 Shari' Filastin; tel: 066-323 5289

Military Museum

🕐 Sat–Thu 9–4 ☎ 066-322 4657 🖐 Inexpensive

Sinai

Sinai sits between Africa and Asia, a place of rugged landscapes and natural beauty. While most of its coastline is being developed into beach resorts and diving centres, the interior remains a desolate mountain desert with some important Christian holy places and Bedouin communities struggling to maintain traditions.

DAHAB

Dahab (Arabic for gold), with its superb beaches and coral reefs, is still considered one of Sinai's best dive sites. The town divides into the Bedouin settlement of Al Asala, the upmarket hotels of Al Mashraba and the camps of Al Masbat, where backpackers and old hippies hang out. It may be the most relaxed town in Egypt, but beware of bathing topless, which is illegal, and of drugs, still widely available although the police are getting tougher. Bedouins organize camel treks into the magnificent desert interior, but Dahab's main sights are undoubtedly under the water, particularly at the Blue Hole and the Canyon (➤ 66).

➕ 12F ✉ 100km (62 miles) northeast of Sharm el Sheikh, 570km (354 miles) from Cairo 🚌 Regular buses from Sharm el Sheikh, Taba, Nuweiba, Cairo

DEIR SANT KATARIN (ST CATHERINE'S MONASTERY)

Best places to see ➤ 42–43.

NUWEIBA

Nuweiba was a thriving resort during the Israeli occupation but now it's a dull and ugly town that attracts few visitors, except

those heading north, or leaving from the port to take the ferry to Aqaba (Jordan). The beaches between Dahab and Nuweiba, now part of the Ras Abu Gallum Protectorate, are spectacular, but the decline in Israeli tourism explains the many unfinished resort hotels along the coastline north of the town. Nuweiba is, however, the best place to arrange camel treks or jeep safaris into the canyons and oases of the Sinai mountains.

➕ 12E ✉ 72km (45 miles) north of Dahab 🚌 Regular buses from Cairo, Sharm el Sheikh, Dahab, Suez and Taba ⛴ Daily fast ferry to Aqaba (Jordan); slow ferry at noon

RAS MUHAMMAD

Ras Muhammad, Sinai's southernmost tip, was declared Egypt's first national park in 1988. The part of the park that can be visited tends to be overwhelmed by daytrippers from Sharm el Sheikh during high season. Its sandstone mountains, *wadis* (dry gullies) and soft sand dunes are inhabited by foxes, gazelles, ibexes and migratory birds.

The stunning coral reefs are a famous haunt for manta rays, sharks and hawksbill turtles, while the magnificent mangroves are breeding grounds for migratory and resident birds.

➕ 18H ✉ 30km (18 miles) from Sharm el Sheikh 🕐 Sunrise–sunset; camping permits issued by visitors' centre Sat–Thu 10am–sunset 🖐 Expensive 🍴 Restaurant (£–££) ❓ Taxis or organized tours. Passport and visa needed for UN checkpoints

SHARM EL SHEIKH

During the Israeli occupation from 1967 to 1982, Sharm el Sheikh was developed mostly for military purposes, but in the last decades it has grown into Egypt's main resort. The Naama Bay area has the highest concentration of hotels and restaurants, but the resort has now spread over several bays. Off the coast and in nearby Ras Muhammad (➤ 175) are some of the most beautiful coral reefs and diving sites in the world, one of the resort's main

attractions. Most hotels offer a wide range of diving and other watersports facilities. The only sight is Ras Kennedy, a rock resembling the former US president John F Kennedy's face.

18H · 470km (292 miles) from Cairo · Buses from Cairo, Dahab, Nuweiba, Suez and Taba · From Cairo and Luxor · High-speed ferry to Hurghada (90 mins) on Mon, Thu and Sat at 5pm, Wed 3pm (often cancelled in winter)

TABA

Taba, a small beach resort on the border with Israel, was returned to Egypt in 1989 after ten years of negotiations. The coastline is beautiful with bays, coves, lagoons and an island. On Geziret al Faraun (Pharaoh's Island) is the 12th-century fortress of Salah al Din, the most important Islamic monument on the Sinai peninsula.

12D · 390km (242 miles) from Cairo · Daily buses from Cairo and Sharm el Sheikh · Flights from Cairo to Ras al Naqb airport

Red Sea Coast

Ancient Egyptians looked for gold, copper and precious stones in
the Red Sea mountains, while early Coptic saints Anthony and
Paul took refuge here from Roman persecutors and in due course
founded the world's first monasteries. Today much of the 1,600km
(994 miles) of coast from Suez to the border of Sudan, with its
beautiful sandy coves and magnificent coral reefs, is being
developed into beach resorts and its fragile habitat is increasingly
coming under threat.

AL GHARDAQA (HURGHADA)

Hurghada has developed fast, from a tiny fishing village into one of Egypt's most popular destinations. The town and its tourist bazaar are of little interest, but large beach resorts offering a variety of watersports make up for that. The water is warm for much of the year and there is a cooling breeze in the hot summers. For those not into diving or snorkelling there is the Sindbad Submarine (tel: 065-344 4688; www.sindbad-group.com), a small Red Sea Aquarium (tel: 065-354 8557) and the beaches.

🚩 17J ✉ 529km (329 miles) southeast of Cairo 🚌 Daily buses from Cairo, Luxor, Aswan and Suez ✈ Flights from Cairo, Luxor, Sharm el Sheikh 🚢 Ferry to Sharm el Sheikh (tel: 065-344 7577) 🛈 On Resort Strip; tel: 065-344 4420

AL GOUNA

Self-contained upmarket resort with several large hotels, a residential area with holiday homes for wealthy Cairenes, an 18-hole golf course and several very pleasant lagoons. Al Gouna has its own airport, an aquarium and a small museum with good replicas of ancient Egyptian treasures.

www.elgouna.com

🚩 17J ✉ 30km (18 miles) north of Hurghada 🚌 Taxis from Hurghada; buses from Cairo three times daily

AL QUSEYR (QUSEIR)

The largest port on the Red Sea until the tenth century, the sleepy town of Quseir, overlooked by a 16th-century fort, offers a welcome alternative to the crowds of Hurghada. There is wonderful snorkelling off the beaches and this is a good base from which to explore the deep south.

🚩 18L ✉ 80km (50 miles) south of Hurghada 🚌 Buses from Cairo, Marsa Alam and Hurghada

HOTELS

SUEZ ZONE

Mercure Forsan Island (££)

By far the best and most peaceful hotel in Ismailia, with comfortable rooms, private beach with watersports and good views over Crocodile Lake.

✉ Forsan Island, 1.5km (1 mile) southeast of Ismailia ☎ 064-391 6316; www.mercure.com

SINAI

Basata (£)

Very popular eco-friendly camp with huts and bungalows on the beach. Those who stay here enjoy the totally relaxed atmosphere. Meals are healthy, natural and communal, there is a desalination plant, and preservation of the coral reefs is high on the agenda.

✉ Ras al Burg on the Taba–Nuweiba road, 42km (26 miles) south of Taba ☎ 069-350 0480/1; www.basata.com

Dahab Paradise (££)

A new hotel built in an architectural style inspired by local traditions, right on the beach facing the Gulf of Aqaba. The hotel has comfortable well-kept rooms, a swimming pool in the garden and a good restaurant.

✉ Beach Dahab ☎ 010-700 2527; www.dahabparadise.com

Four Seasons Sharm el Sheikh (£££)

Moorish-style super-luxurious resort hotel with all facilities, including pools, watersports and a spa. The rooms are set in lush gardens overlooking the Tiran Straits.

✉ Just north of Naama Bay ☎ 069-360 3555; www.fourseasons.com

Moon Beach (££)

Holiday resort with simple, comfortable rooms, away from the crowds, with excellent windsurfing facilities.

✉ At Km98 sign on the road from Ras Sudr to Al Tor, 290km from Sharm el Sheikh, 190km (118 miles) from Cairo ☎ 062-581 0888; www.moonbeachretreat.com

Mövenpick Sharm el Sheikh (£££)

Huge family resort, popular with European package tourists, with bungalows set in a quiet garden, a large swimming pool and all watersports facilities. Kids' entertainment club.

✉ Naama Bay, Sharm el Sheikh ☎ 069-360 0100; www.jolieville-hotels.com

Seven Heaven (£)

Full range of spotless, newly refurbished accommodation from simple huts to rooms with bathroom and ceiling fan. The complex includes a diving centre, internet cafe and restaurant.

✉ Masbat, Dahab ☎ 069-364 0080; www.7heavenhotel.com

RED SEA
Captain's Inn (££)

Smaller hotel with charming rooms set around a peaceful courtyard, overlooking the lagoon. Popular with young Cairenes.

✉ Kafr al Gouna ☎ 065-358 0170; www.captainsinn.elgouna.com

Dawar al Omda (££)

Beautiful hotel built in a modern interpretation of traditional Nile-valley architecture, tastefully decorated with antiques and modern furniture designed by young Cairene designers.

✉ Kafr al Gouna ☎ 065-358 0063; www.dawarelomda-elgouna.com

Al Giftun Beach Resort (££)

One of the oldest holiday resorts, with all facilities for windsurfers and divers. Comfortable bungalows are set on the beach. Several bars and restaurants and all watersports are available.

✉ Resort strip, Hurghada ☎ 065-346 3040; www.giftunbeachresort.com

Miramar Sheraton (£££)

Architect Michael Graves designed the Miramar on several islands around a lagoon, facing the sea. There is a touch of Disney to the buildings, though the interior design owes much to the Mediterranean. Watersports and a golf course.

✉ Al Gouna ☎ 065-354 5606; www.starwoodhotels.com/sheraton

Mövenpick Sirena Beach (£££)

Peaceful hotel, beautifully designed, with spartan, Nubian-style domed rooms and excellent service. Perfect retreat, with some of Egypt's best snorkelling and diving off the hotel's private beach.

✉ Al Quadim Bay, 7km (4 miles) north of Quseir ☎ 065-333 2100; www.moevenpick-quseir.com

Shaqra Ecolodge (££)

Owner Helmy, a lawyer, environmentalist and enthusiastic diver, has set up a small eco-friendly resort with spotlessly clean and comfortable tents, huts and chalets. Mainly aimed at divers, but non-divers looking for peace and quiet will enjoy this place as well.

✉ Marsa Shaqara, 20km (12 miles) north of Marsa Alam ☎ 02-337 1833; www.redsea-divingsafari.com

RESTAURANTS

AL GHARDAQA (HURGHADA)

Felfela (£–££)

Branch of the popular Cairene chain serving good and reasonably priced Egyptian fare.

✉ Shari' Sheraton ☎ 065-442 410 ⊙ Lunch, dinner

Italian Restaurant (££–£££)

Delicious and inventive Italian dishes, including home-made pastas and tender *involtini* (stuffed veal rolls), are served on a romantic garden terrace.

✉ InterContinental Hurghada Hotel ☎ 065-446 911 ⊙ Dinner

Portofino (££)

Italian fish and seafood specialities as well as fresh home-made pasta are served in this pleasant Italian restaurant.

✉ Shari' Sayyed al Qorayem, Al Dahar ☎ 065-354 6250 ⊙ Lunch, dinner

AL GOUNA

Kiki's Italian Cuisine (££)

Popular restaurant with two open-air terraces offering great views over the town and one of the main lagoons. The food is excellent with fresh home-made pastas, ostrich steaks and salads.

✉ Above the museum in Kafr al Gouna ☎ 065-354 2407 🕐 Dinner

Sayyadin Fish Restaurant (££)

Airy and spacious fish restaurant on the beach, with a large terrace, serving excellent fish and seafood.

✉ Mövenpick Hotel, on the beach ☎ 065-354 5160 🕐 Lunch, dinner

Le Tabasco (££)

Branch of the funky Cairene bar-restaurant with excellent Mediterranean food, great music and modern Egyptian decor.

✉ Near the museum, Kafr al Gouna ☎ 065-545 515 🕐 Lunch, dinner

SHARM EL SHEIKH

Al Fanar (££)

The name means lighthouse and that is where this open-air upmarket restaurant is located, at the foot of Sharm's lighthouse. Good Italian food and excellent sea views.

✉ Ras Um Sid ☎ 069-336 2218

Fish Restaurant (£££)

Quiet outdoor fish restaurant, decorated with fishing nets and other fishing paraphernalia, serving excellent French fish and seafood dishes. Service can be erratic.

✉ Near diving centre, Hilton Fayrouz, Naama Bay ☎ 069-360 0137
🕐 Dinner only

Hard Rock Café (£–££)

Casual atmosphere and the usual memorabilia, which belonged to rock stars such as Madonna, Elton John and Elvis Presley.

✉ Shari' Sultan Qaboos, Naama Bay ☎ 062-360 2664 🕐 12:30pm–2am (4am at weekends)

Pirates Bar (££)

Popular venue for an evening drink, in a romantic garden with bridges over little ponds. Happy hour 5:30–7:30.

✉ Hilton Fayrouz, Naama Bay ☎ 069-360 0137 🕐 Evening

La Rustichella (££)

One of the best Italian restaurants in town, very popular with the large Italian contingent, serving Italian food as only "la mamma" can cook it. Great choice of pastas. Book in advance.

✉ Behind Naama Bay ☎ 069-360 1154 🕐 Lunch, dinner

Sala Thai (££–£££)

Excellent Thai restaurant with modern Asian decor and a lovely terrace overlooking the sea.

✉ Hyatt Regency Hotel, Naama Bay ☎ 069-360 1234 🕐 Dinner

TamTam (£–££)

Large menu with simple but excellent Egyptian food served in this popular indoor restaurant or on the more pleasant terrace.

✉ Ghazala Hotel, Naama Bay ☎ 069-360 0150 🕐 Lunch, dinner

SUEZ ZONE
George's (££)

Cairenes come for the day to sample George's famous fish and seafood in this Greek-run restaurant.

✉ 1 Shari et Thawra, Ismailia ☎ 064-391 8327 🕐 Lunch, dinner

SHOPPING

HANDICRAFTS
Aladin

This is a tiny shop with small antiques, Bedouin textiles and a good selection of glass beads, scarabs and hand-carved sea urchin bones.

✉ In the Al Diar Hotel, Naama Bay, Sharm el Sheikh ☎ 062-360 0826

Fansina

Fansina sells the beautiful embroidery work they commission from 460 Bedouin women belonging to the four tribes who live around St Catherine. This successful project is supported by the European Union and keeps on growing.

✉ Shari' al Rasees, St Catherine ☎ 010-1865 120/069-3470 155; www.fansina.net

ENTERTAINMENT

NIGHTLIFE

Alf Layla wa Layla

As close to Disneyland as you can get in this region, where you can have dinner amid over-the-top decor while watching a good belly-dance show.

✉ Safaga Road, Hurghada ☎ 065 346 4601

Black House Disco

Lively night venue with international DJs, but less crowded than Pacha (► below).

✉ Rosetta Hotel, Naama Bay, Sharm el Sheikh ☎ 069-360 1888

Clubhouse

This is where Al Gouna's young crowd hangs out all day and all night, with loud music, DJs, a swimming pool and a private beach. Stay away if you don't like loud music. If you happen to be here during an Egyptian holiday, then this is where the wild parties take place.

✉ Al Gouna

Hard Rock Café

See page 183.

Pacha

The first-ever Pacha club in the Middle East and Africa, and one of the most popular nightspots in town.

✉ Sanafir Hotel, Naama Bay, Sharm el Sheikh ☎ 069-600 0197

Papa Beach Club

Always filled to the brim, this popular beach club has some of the wildest parties in town, with European DJ. Check the website for special nights, including karaoke and big-screen TV events.

✉ Sigala, Hurghada ☎ www.papasbar.com

Pirates Bar

See page 183.

Index

Acknowledgements

The Automobile Association would like to thank the following photographers, companies and picture libraries for their assistance in the preparation of this book.

Abbreviations for the picture credits are as follows – (t) top; (b) bottom; (c) centre; (l) left; (r) right; (AA) AA World Travel Library.

4l Sphinx, AA/C Sawyer; **4c** Bus, Cairo, AA/C Sawyer; **4r** Pyramid and Great Sphinx, Giza, AA/C Sawyer; **5l** Market, AA/C Sawyer; **5c** TV Tower, Cairo, AA/C Sawyer; **6/7** Sphinx, AA/C Sawyer; **8/9** Souvenirs, Khan al Khalili bazaar, Cairo, AA/C Sawyer; **10/11t** Two Colossi of Amenophis III, Luxor, AA/R Strange; **10cl** Horse and carriage carrying tourists, Giza, AA/C Sawyer; **10cr** Bedouin girl, Siwa Oasis, AA/R Strange; **10b** Agricultural worker, Dahshur, AA/C Sawyer; **11tl** Salah Salem Avenue, Cairo, AA/C Sawyer; **11tr** Bahariya Oasis, man on donkey, AA/C Coe; **11cr** Manyal Palace, Cairo, AA/C Coe; **11cb** Museum of Antiquities, Cairo, AA/C Coe; **11b** High Dam at Aswan, AA/C Coe; **12/13t** Street vendor, Cairo, AA/C Sawyer; **12c** Plate of deep-fried aubergines, AA/C Sawyer; **12b** Mezze, Cairo, AA/C Sawyer; **13t** Fresh fish for sale, Cairo, AA/C Sawyer; **13c** Pigs' trotters and sheep head for sale, Cairo, AA/C Sawyer;

13b Pastries and cakes for sale, Cairo, AA/C Sawyer; **14t** Street vendor, AA/C Sawyer; **14c** Umm Ali dessert, Cairo, AA/C Sawyer; **14/15t** Tewifiqiya fruit and veg market, Cairo, AA/C Sawyer; **15** Mezze, Cairo, AA/C Sawyer; **16/17** Pyramids, Giza, AA/C Sawyer; **16c** Two snorkellers, AA/C Sawyer; **16b** Camel and riders, Giza, AA/C Sawyer; **17l** Shoes outside Amr ibn al As Mosque, Cairo, AA/C Sawyer; **17r** Felucca, Cairo, AA/C Sawyer; **18** Khan al Khalili bazaar, Cairo, AA/C Sawyer; **18/19t** Museum of Ancient Egyptian Art, Luxor, AA/R Strange; **18/19b** Statue of Yamu-Nedjeh, Museum of Ancient Egyptian Art, Luxor, AA/R Strange; **19** Statue of Ramses II, Luxor, AA/R Strange; **20/21** Bus, Cairo, AA/C Sawyer; **27** Mar Girgist Metro line, Cairo, AA/C Sawyer; **28** Taxi, Cairo, AA/C Sawyer; **30/31** Telephone box, Cairo, AA/C Sawyer; **34/35** Pyramid and Great Sphinx, Giza, AA/C Sawyer; **36** Temple of Seti, Abydos, AA/R Strange; **36/37** Temple of Seti, Abydos, AA/R Strange; **37** Relief carving, Temple of Seti, Abydos, AA/R Strange; **38/39** Camel and riders, Giza, AA/R Strange; **40** Tomb of Seti I, Valley of the Kings, AA/R Strange; **40/41** Valley of the Kings, Luxor, AA/R Strange; **41** Tomb of Seti I, Valley of the Kings, AA/R Strange; **42** Monastery of St Catherine, Mount Sinai, AA/C Coe; **42/43** Icon of St Catherine, Monastery, Mount Sinai, AA/C Coe; **43** Monastery of St Catherine, Mount Sinai, AA/C Coe; **44** Temple of Amun, Karnak, AA/R Strange; **44/45** Avenue of Sphinxes, Temple of Amun, Karnak, AA/C Coe; **45** Hieroglyphics at Karnak, AA/C Coe; **46/47t** Restaurants, Khan al Khalili bazaar, Cairo, AA/C Sawyer; **46/47b** Khan al Khalili bazaar, Cairo, AA/C Sawyer; **48** Jewels from Tutankhamun's tomb, Egyptian Museum of Antiquities, Cairo, AA/C Coe; **48/49** Egyptian Museum of Antiquities, Cairo, AA/C Sawyer; **49** Death Mask of Tutankhamun, Egyptian Museum of Antiquities, Cairo, AA/C Sawyer; **50** Boats on Nile, Cairo, AA/C Sawyer; **50/51** Cruise ships, Nile Valley ©4Corners Images/Johanna Huber/SIME; **52** Reliefs, Temple of Isis, Philae, AA/R Strange; **52/53** Temple of Isis, Philae, AA/C Coe; **53** Kiosk of Trajan, Temple of Isis, Philae, AA/R Strange; **54/55** Sultan Hasan Mosque-Madrasa, Cairo, AA/C Sawyer; **55** Sultan Hasan Mosque-Madrasa, Cairo, AA/H Alexander; **56/57** Market, AA/C Sawyer; **58/59** Mezze, AA/C Sawyer; **60/61** Horse riding, Giza, AA/C Sawyer; **62/63** Al Muski Market, Cairo, AA/C Sawyer; **64/65** Mount Catherine and Mount Sinai, AA/R Strange; **66/67** Snorkeller, AA/C Sawyer; **69** Children, Cairo, AA/C Sawyer; **70/71** Brassworker, Khan al Khalili bazaar, Cairo, AA/R Strange; **72** Feluccas, Nile, AA/R Strange; **72/73** Feluccas, Nile, AA/C Coe; **75** Coptic papyrus, Coptic Museum, Cairo, AA/C Coe; **76/77** TV Tower, Cairo, AA/C Sawyer; **79** Amr ibn el As Mosque, Cairo, AA/C Sawyer; **80** Amr ibn el As Mosque, Cairo, AA/C Sawyer; **81** Amr ibn el As Mosque, Cairo, AA/C Sawyer; **82/83** Mosque of Al Muayyad, Cairo, AA/C Sawyer; **84** Mosque of Al Hakim, AA/C Sawyer; **86** Bayt al Suhaymi Mansion, Cairo, AA/C Sawyer; **86/87t** Bayt al Suhaymi, Cairo, AA/C Sawyer; **86/87b** Ben Ezra Synagogue, Cairo, AA/C Sawyer; **88** Gezira Island, AA/C Sawyer; **88/89** Al Azhar Park, Nico Tondini/Robert Harding; **91** Mr and Mrs Mahmoud Khalil Museum, Cairo, AA/C Sawyer; **92/3** El Muallaqa, AA/C Sawyer; **94** Citadel, Cairo, AA/C Coe; **94/95** Barquq Mosque, Cairo, AA/C Sawyer; **96** Qaytbay Mausoleum-Madrasa, Cairo, AA/C Sawyer; **96/97** Downtown Cairo, AA/C Sawyer; **98/99** Pyramids, Dahshur, AA/C Sawyer; **100** Solar Boat, Giza, AA/R Strange; **101** Statue of Ramses II, Memphis, AA/R Strange; **102/103** Step Pyramid, Saqqara, AA/C Sawyer; **117** Bahariya Oasis, AA/C Coe; **118** Pompey's Pillar, Alexandria, AA/C Coe; **119** Pompey's Pillar, Alexandria, AA/R Strange; **120** Kom al Shogafa Catacombs, Alexandria, AA/C Coe; **121** Kom al Shogafa Catacombs, Alexandria, AA/R Strange; **122/123** Kom al Dikka, Alexandria, AA/R Strange; **124** Alexandria National Museum, ©Danita Delimont/Alamy; **125** Montazah Palace, Alexandria, AA/R Strange; **126/127** Qaytbay Fort, Alexandria, AA/R Strange; **127** British and Commonwealth Cemetery, Al Alamein, AA/R Strange; **128/129** Rosetta Stone, AA/C Coe; **130/131** Dakhla Oasis, Photolibrary; **132** Shali Village, Siwa Oasis, AA/R Strange; **139** Karnak, AA/H Alexander; **140/141** Temple of Luxor, AA/R Strange; **141t** Madinat Habu Temple, Luxor, AA/H Alexander; **141b** Madinat Habu Temple, Luxor, AA/H Alexander; **143** Luxor Temple, AA/H Alexander; **144/145** Museum of Ancient Egyptian Art, Luxor, AA/R Strange; **146** Tomb of the Nobles, Photolibrary; **147** Mortuary Temple of Queen Hatshepsut, AA/R Strange; **149** Valley of the Kings, AA/R Strange; **150** Colossus of Ramses II, Valley of the Kings, AA/R Strange; **151** Tombs at Beni Hasan, AA/R Strange; **152/153t** Tell al Amarna, AA/R Strange; **152/153b** Tell al Amarna, AA/R Strange; **154/5** Mausoleum of Aga Khan, AA/R Strange; **156** Unfinished Obelisk, Aswan, AA/C Coe; **156/157** High Dam Monument, Aswan Dam, AA/C Coe; **158** The Jabberwock, Temple of Horus, Edfu, AA/R Strange; **159** Temple of Horus, Edfu, AA/R Strange; **160** Roman Temple of Khnum, Esna, AA/R Strange; **161** Ptolemaic Temple, Kom Ombo, AA/R Strange; **162/163** Statue of Ramses, Temple of Ra-Herakhte, Abu Simnel, AA/R Strange; **164** Temple of Kalabsha, Aswan, AA/C Coe; **171** Sharm el Sheikh, AA/R Strange; **172** Suez Canal, Port Said, AA/R Strange; **172/173** Port Said, AA/R Strange; **173** Port Said, AA/R Strange; **174** Gulf of Aqaba, AA/R Strange; **175** Nuweiba, Gulf of Aqaba, AA/R Strange; **176/177** Sharm al Sheikh, ©Eric Gevaert/Alamy; **178/179** Diver, AA/J Holmes.

Every effort has been made to trace the copyright holders, and we apologise in advance for any unintentional omissions or errors. We would be pleased to apply any corrections in a following edition of this publication.

Sight locator index

This index relates to the maps on the covers. We have given map references to the main sights in the book. Grid references in italics indicate sights featured on the town plan. Some sights within towns may not be plotted on the maps.

Dear Reader

Your comments, opinions and recommendations are very important to us. Please help us to improve our travel guides by taking a few minutes to complete this simple questionnaire.

You do not need a stamp (unless posted outside the UK). If you do not want to cut this page from your guide, then photocopy it or write your answers on a plain sheet of paper.

Send to: **The Editor, AA World Travel Guides,**
FREEPOST SCE 4598, Basingstoke RG21 4GY.

Your recommendations...

We always encourage readers' recommendations for restaurants, nightlife or shopping – if your recommendation is used in the next edition of the guide, we will send you a **FREE AA Guide** of your choice from this series. Please state below the establishment name, location and your reasons for recommending it.

_____
_____
_____
_____
_____
_____

Please send me **AA Guide** _____

About this guide...

Which title did you buy?

AA _____

Where did you buy it? _____

When? m m / y y

Why did you choose this guide? _____

_____
_____
_____
_____

Did this guide meet your expectations?

Exceeded ☐   Met all ☐   Met most ☐   Fell below ☐

Were there any aspects of this guide that you particularly liked? _____

_____
_____
_____

continued on next page...

Is there anything we could have done better? _____

_____

_____

_____

About you...
Name (Mr/Mrs/Ms) _____

Address _____

_____

_____ Postcode _____

Daytime tel nos _____

Email _____

Please only give us your mobile phone number or email if you wish to hear from us about
other products and services from the AA and partners by text or mms, or email.

Which age group are you in?
Under 25 ☐   25–34 ☐   35–44 ☐   45–54 ☐   55–64 ☐   65+ ☐

How many trips do you make a year?
Less than one ☐   One ☐   Two ☐   Three or more ☐

Are you an AA member? Yes ☐   No ☐

About your trip...
When did you book? m m / y y   When did you travel? m m / y y

How long did you stay? _____

Was it for business or leisure? _____

Did you buy any other travel guides for your trip? _____

If yes, which ones? _____

_____

_____

Thank you for taking the time to complete this questionnaire. Please send it to us as soon as
possible, and remember, you do not need a stamp (unless posted outside the UK).

> **AA** Travel Insurance call 0800 072 4168 or visit www.theAA.com